Beating the Squeeze
Financial Planning During a Recession

Beating the Squeeze
Financial Planning During a Recession

Anthony Vice

www.emeraldpublishing.co.uk

CONTENTS

Introduction

INTRODUCTION

Beating the squeeze, in this book, means how to keep up your lifestyle even when that is being made more difficult by government actions. Some people, when faced by the squeeze, will make economies-take a cheaper holiday, put off buying the fridge. That is one way to react, but then you are not beating the squeeze, you are accepting it.

To beat the squeeze means taking a few major decisions and then adopting a slightly different attitude of mind. Beating the squeeze does not mean that you have to acquire a mass of technical knowledge nor have to spend your spare time going over sheets of financial figures. The major decisions, described in the following chapters, involve, say, looking at who holds the unit trust and savings account, thinking about tracker funds and using a discount broker for a fund platform when you buy an ISA.

Your new attitude of mind means being alert to new ways in which you can get better value for the pound you spend or how what you are doing can be made to cost less. No bell rings when you make a brilliant, or mistaken, financial decision. Unless you hire a financial adviser, and give him a wide brief, there is no one else looking out after you. Just lack of knowledge can be a major problem- such as knowing which credit card to use outside the UK, and why?

All this is not made any easier because the finance business changes rapidly- and there is no simple way to find out what these changes are and how that might affect you. Pensions are an important issue for most people, where the law has been changed drastically over the last few years. (and is about to change again).

If you do not keep up, you may lose out and you could even, unintentionally, commit some technical mistake.

It comes down to your own reaction- you may accept the squeeze and adapt your lifestyle to the financial pressures. On the other hand, you may decide to fight back and use the financial system prevent the squeeze from altering the way you live and work. If you are one of the second group, read on.

****

1

MANAGE CREDIT CARDS

Credit cards are the way, in a financial squeeze, to access significant amounts of cash at low cost. They have to be one of the best ways to beat a squeeze- but you have to manage them. Your objective: to borrow your entire credit limit, which could be several thousand pounds, for about three years, and pay 1% a year.

Sounds good? Here is how you get there.

You will face a problem with credit cards if you have a patchy credit record, i.e. if you pay late or spend more than your credit card limit. If you have had issues with card companies in the past, then your first step is to re-establish a sound credit history. To do this, you should take out a new card and, for at least a year, manage it by the book: you stay within your credit limit and you always pay the card bill on time.

If you have questions about your credit record, go to an agency such as Equifax. For just £2 they will send you a copy of your credit history- which is the first thing a credit card company will look at when you apply to them. You may see a mistake: if you do, you have the legal right to get it corrected.

USE DIRECT DEBIT

You will also face money costs: one of the leading cards will charge you £12 for any default charge (which means paying late) going over your credit limit or having a payment bounce back (say when you set up a direct debit to pay monthly bills there was not enough money in the account). Card companies will take payment in several ways but the best is a direct debit through your bank. This is virtually 100% safe, the bill will be paid on time, and if it does go wrong then it becomes the bank's fault- not yours.

The card company will not be at all upset if you borrow from them- when you do not pay the full amount of your outstanding monthly bill or maybe just pay the minimum, say £5 or 2% of the total bill. You are the one who should be upset, because you will be paying a stiff rate of interest, anywhere between 15% and 25% on what you borrow (remember: if you pay 25%, that will compound so that what you owe will treble in five years)

YOU MAY NEED RE-FINANCE

Borrowing occasionally is one thing, but you simply cannot afford to borrow from a credit card on a regular basis. You need to step back and re-finance your card borrowing- which means you go for a bank loan or overdraft or raise money from your house through equity release.

Some card companies will offer you credit card cheques, where the cheque amount is debited to your card. Credit card cheques are best avoided: they may carry a fee and whatever you spend is likely to be charged interest from the date of the transaction.

KNOW THE DATE

So you have your credit card and you are a savvy card user.
means that you know the date of your monthly statement (sc
card companies allow you to fix your own date when you appl,
and you make any large purchase just after that date rather than
just before- this buys you an extra month's credit. You also know
to use a debit card, not a credit card, to draw cash. Using a credit
card, you will probably pay a fee and be charged interest from the
date you took the money.

You also know to use your credit card when you make any big
deal-a new TV or package holiday. Most people are familiar with
Consumer Credit legislation, which makes the credit card
company responsible, with the seller, for any faults or
misrepresentation on a deal worth between £100 and £30,000.
Remember that this cover applies abroad, but also remember that
charge cards- where you pay the bill in full each month- are not
covered, nor is anything you buy with a debit card or credit card
cheque.

There has to be a credit element. In that case, if what you ordered
is faulty, or not delivered, or the supplier goes broke, you can
look to the credit card company for compensation.

CHOOSE CASHBACK

A number of people manage to pay all of their credit card bills in
full every month. If you are one of them, you have a further
choice. You can choose a cashback card, which does what it says
on the tin.

When this was written, Amex and Capital One were the two leaders: you may get an introductory offer (say 5% back on whatever you spend for three months up to £100) and after that are handed back between 0.5% and 1.25% depending on the total you spend- the card company generally takes it off your bill once a year.(Be aware: some of the better deals are aimed at new customers, so if you already hold the card, you may not get new cashback terms)

The banks are also moving into cashback: you pay for an account, maybe get some interest plus a return of cash on certain types of transactions. You will be expected to settle those transactions by direct debit (so the bank can log how you spend) and pay your monthly salary into the account.

OR SHOP VOUCHERS

Cash has an obvious appeal, but some companies offer air miles or points which you can spend at specified retailers. Shop groups such as Tesco and Waitrose have their own cards; they send you vouchers every few months which you can use in-store.

Many card users will be able to collect a couple of hundred pounds over a year in this way- but there is one caution. The value of the cashback will be lost if you do not pay the full amount of your bill each month. The margin on cashback is small, making it useful rather than a major financial play.

BUYING AT 0%

Credit cards offer two major financial plays, which together will give you your three-year money at low cost. These are 0%

purchases and balance transfers. As you are a safe and sound card user, these are open to you to access. 0% purchases mean just what they say; for up to 18 months, you can buy whatever you want without having to pay for the credit. There are just two, minor, constraints; you have to stay within your credit limit and each month you will have to make the minimum repayments, say £5 or 2% of what you owe. Just think what you are getting; if your credit limit is £3,000, then you have an interest-free loan of that amount. The only difference between the various companies' 0% cards is how long the interest-free period lasts

NEW CUSTOMERS TARGETED

Nor is it that difficult to find 0% purchase cards-details appear on the net and in newspapers. But you have to remember that these cards are targeted at new customers, so you may be accepted for 0% purchases if you already hold that particular card or have held it some time over the past year. It should not be too hard to find a 0% purchase deal for which you are eligible- but avoid the beginner's mistake of applying for a number of cards at the same time. If you make multiple applications, they will all appear on your credit history and that will not look good- card companies may wonder if you are planning a scam or a spending binge, or whether you expect many of your card applications to be rejected. Do a little homework first and apply for the most appealing card.

WHEN TIME RUNS OUT- ARRANGE A BALANCE TRANSFER

So you enjoy your interest-free loan for say 18 months. You have made a great series of purchases, running into several thousand pounds, which have cost you zero interest and where you have only had to pay back the small minimum amount each month. But as the end of the 18 months gets near, you accept that the card company will want to be paid back. What do you do?

What you do is arrange a balance transfer to another 12-18 months, so doubling the life of your loan. In principle, this could not be simpler- you transfer the balance, i.e. your debt, from your present card to a new one. You should be able to get a deal for 0% interest over the life of the loan, but there will be a fee: typically around 3% of the debt which you transfer. This is the only cost to you of the entire three years operation. In that way, you will have borrowed several thousand pounds (your entire credit limit) for three years at a cost of 1% a year. A way to beat the squeeze!

MAYBE ANOTHER TRANSFER?

Unless the world changes, you may be able to arrange another balance transfer when your first one expires-provided that you can carry the necessary portfolio of cards. But if you can make that work, you would be paying 3% for a sizeable 18-month loan. Just compare that interest rate with what a bank or a short-term lender would charge you-or what the credit card company would charge you for cash.

But suppose that you want to use a credit card while the balance transfer operates? Probably the best answer is to use another card. This used to be a finance minefield, with the card companies using your cash to pay off the low-cost debt and leave you with the higher-rate. The rules have now been changed, so that debt must be paid off with higher-rate first, but a new card would be simpler-assuming, again, that you can carry the portfolio of cards that you will need.

CARDS FROM STORES

Credit cards have become so popular that many retailers and internet sellers have created their own, which are likely to be offered to you without your needing to ask. Store cards typically offer useful cash inducements-you get price reduction if you sign up for the card on the spot. These price reductions are often worth having, but beware: store cards charge even higher interest rates than the national cards. The answer has to be- take the price reduction, but make certain that you pay off the monthly bill in full.

You will find credit cards, especially Visa, Master-card and American Express used in most countries throughout the world-so when you go abroad, you take you own card to use in ATMs, shops and restaurants and to pay your hotel bill. Pause- this may be the best cost-saving idea!

PAY TO CONVERT

If you just take your card, you are likely to pay significantly more than you need in commissions and deductions. For the detailed answer, look at the chapter on how to plan your holiday spend, but keep in mind the one key issue: most cards will charge you a commission when they convert your holiday spend from dollars, euros or whatever back to sterling to make up your monthly bill. There are just a few cards which do not make this charge, and these are the cards which you should take on holiday.

Another type of card to take on holiday is the loaded card (see the holiday chapter for detail) but that is also widely used elsewhere. Reverse the key idea which led to the creation of the credit card: with a loaded card, you put money onto the card, then draw it down through ATMs, shops and restaurants. No bank is involved, as you just get out what you put in. That makes it easier to apply for a loaded card than for a card which gives you credit-though remember that no credit means no consumer protection.

WAYS TO MOVE MONEY

You can budget with a loaded card and there is no way that you can spend more than you put in. There is also a security benefit: if a villain gets hold of your card, the maximum amount you could lose is what you have loaded. As there is no bank involved, he cannot backtrack to your bank account, as he might be able to do with a regular credit card. You can load someone else's card, which makes it an easy way to transfer money to someone-say to a son or daughter at university. You might be able to persuade your employer to pay you by loading your card. If loaded cards appeal to you, you need to check out the cost. There will probably be a charge when you set up the card and when you finally close it down. You will not receive any interest on the money which you have loaded. There may be other costs when you load from a bank or use the card in an ATM. There is a wide choice now among loaded cards, and you need to check just what you will be liable for.

BEWARE OF CROOKS

Credit cards are useful pieces of plastic, which can get lost or stolen and attract crooks. If you lose a card, action is simple: you contact the card company at once and write a note to yourself that you have done so. You may be liable, but only up to the first £50 if someone else uses your card. If you hold a number of cards, you could use one of the companies which will take a list of your cards and tell the card companies if they go missing.

Much more dangerous is when your card is stolen- without ever leaving your wallet. Remember that the crook just needs to know your card number, the card expiry date and your billing address. He could get the data from a waiter in a restaurant who copies your details or from the man behind the bar if you leave your card to run a tab. Even more likely, he will find what he wants from a bill or letter which you yourself have discarded. Your problem here is not so much financial loss as a very great deal of hassle for a period of time –and your card will be out of action until all the issues have been sorted.

Here are 10 simple ideas to help keep you out of trouble:

1. Do not let your card out of your sight.
2. When the card company asks for a password, make one up-your mother's maiden name is in the public domain.
3. When you go, say, to a garage which you do not know, think about paying cash instead of using a card.
4. When you buy over the net (only ever on a secure site) use just one card-preferably one with a low credit limit just in case there is a problem.
5. When you get your monthly statement, read it-if there is anything you do not recognise, phone the card company.
6. When you travel, keep a separate list of card numbers and phone contacts. And tell the card company when you plan to use the card away from home.

2

WHICH FLAVOUR MORTGAGE?

First –time buyers now have the chance of a better mortgage deal. When this was written, they could choose from more than 300 mortgages where the lenders wanted only a 10% deposit-to LTV (loan to value) ratio of 90%. Three years ago, lenders were offering fewer than100 mortgages of this type. Interest rates, too, for first-time buyers are lower as the Bank of England's base rate looks set to stay at 0.5% for another year or so.

But before a borrower decides which flavour mortgage he would like, he has to be sure that his credit record is solid- lenders nowadays can afford to be choosy and lean economic times are likely to make them choosier. And he still has to find the hard cash for the deposit. On a £250.000 house that equals £25,000 plus legal and survey fees and the cost of the move.

On regular Mortgages and re-mortgages, the squeeze means that you will have to find a bigger deposit. Borrowers who are not first-time buyers typically have to find 25% of the total cost, and you will need to put up 40% if you are looking for the best terms in the market.

BANK OF MUM AND DAD

For many people, this points to the Bank of Mum and Dad, where the parents give or lend the money or-rather more sophisticatedly- supply a guarantee. The parents agree to a bank taking a charge over their shares or ISAs, so the bank provides the guarantee which the young couple can use to help buy their house.

Some lenders, noting the trend, have set up schemes to enable parents to provide additional security for first-time buyers. One of the biggest lenders runs a scheme for parents to put money into a savings bond. Another big lender operates a save to buy scheme-as a first-time buyer, you save with them for six months and you can then apply for a 95% mortgage.

The government has unrolled its New-Buy Guarantee Scheme: you can spend up to £500,000 on a new-build property and borrow with a 5% deposit. This works because the scheme protects the mortgage lender if the borrower defaults-the cost is shared between the developer and the taxpayer.

REGULAR VANILLA CHOICE

So which flavour mortgage do you want? The regular vanilla flavour is the repayment mortgage, where the lender sets the rate of interest at his SVR-Standard Variable Rate. A repayment mortgage means that every month you pay both interest and a further amount to help gradually pay off the capital. The SVR which you pay is the lender's standard rate for loans, which is loosely linked to the Bank of England base rate.

Vanilla is fine, but it may not be the cheapest and you need to think about other flavours to suit your own taste. First has to be an interest-only mortgage: you do not make monthly payments off the capital of your debt, but deal with it when the loan comes to end. The difference from a repayment mortgage is simple- you make one payment a month, the interest, instead of two. If you borrow £200,000, a repayment mortgage would today cost you £1,055 a month compared with £666 for an interest-only loan.

With an interest-only mortgage you get a large benefit in terms of current cash flow, but you understand that you will have to find a sizeable lump of cash to pay what you borrowed when the loan comes to an end. Your neighbour, who took a repayment mortgage, will have paid off his debt.

INTEREST-ONLY GET HARDER

The not-so-good news is that interest-only mortgages look like being harder to find. The Financial Services Authority, the City of London's watchdog, is tightening controls on interest-only loans, and the major lenders are following their example. It is not hard to guess at the thinking: many people who chose interest-only mortgages believed that rising house prices, plus perhaps growth in shares held in their ISAs, would wipe out debt. But house prices have been flat over the past five years and shares prices overall are lower than they were 10 years ago.

This is hard on people for whom interest-only makes good sense- say doctors who start on a low income but who could switch to a repayment mortgage when they earn more. Bankers who receive bonuses could also look for an interest-only mortgage, as would many workers who are self-employed. But tougher controls, especially checks on repayment prospects, look all too likely.

MAYBE THINK OFFSET

One type of mortgage has survived the squeeze-which can save money for a borrower, especially if they pay tax at 40%. This is the offset mortgage: its interest rate will be rather higher than on a straightforward mortgage but the offset saves by using your savings to reduce- i.e. offset-the amount you borrow.

Your mortgage, cash and savings all remain separate. But if you have a mortgage of £200,000 and savings of £20,000, you pay interest only on £180,000 which represents the difference. Your savings are offset.

DOUBLE GAIN

You save money in two ways. If you invested your savings, rather than use an offset, you would get a lower rate of interest than you are paying on your mortgage- so paying less mortgage interest means that you come out ahead. Secondly, you would have to pay tax on the interest if you invested separately. It makes sense to pay less interest on your loan rather than earn interest, out of which the taxman will take anything up to 50%.

Offset mortgages work well- though not for everyone. You need to have significant savings- at best 25% or more of your mortgage- for the sums to work and offset the higher than average interest rate. Offset mortgages may not be such a good idea if you have to keep using and then top-up your savings- or if you think you may have to spend them all. If that happened, you would be left with a traditional-type mortgage at a rather high interest rate.

DO YOU FIX OR FLOAT?

You have one other strategic decision to make- which could be very profitable if you get it right. This is whether or not you choose a fixed rate of interest. You can fix for a few years or for the life of the loan. The alternative is to take the lender's SVR or, more likely to opt for a tracker, which will follow every change in the base rate.

Which choice you should make depends on how interest rates will move in the years ahead, over the life of your loan. Sadly, there is no one on earth who can give you a reliable forecast of interest rates over the next 20 years-so you are on your own. Many people go for a compromise-fix for two or three years and then move to a tracker. Whichever type of deal you choose, it is important that you resolve not to look back in later years-"if only" does not help.

LENDERS "COLLAR"

You need to bear two things in mind. One is that a tracker may rise, but there are limits to how far it will fall. When the Bank of England first started to cut interest rates, some lenders introduced a "collar". They added a minimum level for your loan rate-often 2% or 3%-below which it will not fall, whatever happens to base rate.

Secondly, if you choose a fixed rate, take on board that you are getting an extra item- certainty. You know what your interest costs will be for the life of the fix, which (at least for that time) means that changes to base rate, SVR and tracker rates will have no impact on you.

CERTAINTY ON COSTS

This explains why so many people fix for a few years, so they can adjust to their new spending pattern. For someone who can just afford their mortgage payments, certainty on interest costs could be critically important. For them, a sudden jump in interest rates could spell disaster- while anyone with a fixed rate mortgage is protected.

Jargon, you will by now have gathered, is all round the mortgage market, so you need to be up to speed. Terms such as fixed and tracker are clear, and collar, meaning a minimum, is not too hard to follow. The opposite of a collar is a cap, meaning a maximum: this type of mortgage was popular a few years ago, when interest rates were higher. Some lenders still offer capped mortgages- in return for higher interest rate, you get the assurance that the rate of interest will not go above a pre-determined figure.

CASHBACK OR DISCOUNT?

Two other terms you need to follow when applied to mortgages are "cashback" and "discount". With a cashback , you will receive back say several thousand pounds equal to 5% or 10% of your loan. The idea is to help pay all the incidental costs of moving house-as well as legal and surveying fees, there will be the costs of the move itself plus a range of expected, and unexpected, outgoings.

You will probably pay a higher interest rate for a cashback mortgage, but its principal feature will be the penalty if you want to change your mortgage in the following three to five years. Later, you may find a better deal and want to re-mortgage (see the next chapter) but cashback mortgages –with the lender in that situation maybe asking for his money back- are virtually guaranteed to make it too expensive to switch.

REDUCTION ON SVR

Another attractive-looking deal is the discount mortgage, where you are given a reduction on the lender's Standard Variable Rate. You need to be entirely clear on the size of the discount and the level of rate which is being discounted-if these make sense, then go ahead and take your discount You will pay a higher rate of interest than on a standard mortgage and it will be expensive to change your mortgage so long as the discount applies (typically two or three years).

Whether you take a cashback or a discount mortgage (or even a combination) will to depend on your own situation. In effect, with both deals you temporarily give up the right to re-mortgage; you need a crystal ball to know if that will be a disadvantage over the next few years.

MAYBE PAY FOR ADVICE

All this may look like a heavy programme for you, a non-professional financier. Mortgages, along with pensions and some types of insurance, are an area where it often makes sense to go to a broker and pay for advice (remember to include his costs when you do your mortgage budget).

Some mortgage deals are available only through a broker, and he is likely to hear of attractive deals before they get to the public. And if a problem emerges later on, you have an adviser to talk to- or sue if things get really difficult (residential mortgage brokers are regulated by the City's watchdog the Financial Services Authority).

COVER THE UK

Your first thought, when looking for advice, may be to go to your own bank or building society. You should talk to them, but appreciate that they may be what used to be called "tied advisers"- they will advise you only on the products offered by companies within their own financial group. You need a broker who covers the whole of the UK mortgage market, and you should check the scope of their coverage with the brokers you contact.

Tying down the cost is essential when you deal with a broker. You will find a considerable variety: many brokers charge a fee, especially when they offer a face-to-face service, whereas some just take a commission. The broker will expect to get his money when your deal is completed.

****

3

THINK REMORTGAGE

So you get your mortgage. This is by far your biggest debt. In a financial squeeze, you feel that you must be able to get the costs down. How do you do it?

You may have been given a special deal, such as a discount, cashback or capped mortgage, which ended after five years. (Some lenders used to charge 'overhanging' redemption penalties which continued after the benefit stopped (check the paperwork). You now have a standard repayment mortgage and you pay the lender's SVR (Standard Variable Rate). You feel that a new mortgage would help-so think re-mortgage.

CLEAN CREDIT HISTORY

The first question has to be: are you likely to get one? You are going to need a clean credit history and be able to show equity of a minimum 25%, preferably 40% to get the best deal. Your house may have risen in value-house prices, on average, have not shown great change over five years but have doubled if you look over 10 years (regions differ: prices in greater London have risen even over five years). In your favour, your mortgage debt will have come down after five years or more of capital repayments.

You will also find it easier to re-mortgage if your personal situation has improved. Maybe you have got a better job. Maybe your partner is now able to work part-time.

BIGGER LTV

If the numbers look promising, you need to think what you want from a new mortgage. If you are paying Standard Variable Rate which is linked to, but higher than, base rate, you should be able to reduce your interest costs. Alternatively, you may want to borrow more by taking a higher proportion of the improved value of your house- i.e. get a bigger LTV (Loan to Value)

Re-mortgaging could be especially useful if you plan to consolidate your borrowings and cut down higher-rate personal loans on hire purchase debt. Some advisers caution against adding any non-housing debt to your mortgage because your house is the final security. If problems arise, the worst case is that your house is repossessed. Whether or not it makes sense to consolidate your debt will ultimately depend on your total interest costs and on prospects for the family income.

WHEN LESS IS MORE

Alternatively, you may plan to extend the life of your loan: you need to pause and think about this idea. A longer term loan will reduce your current interest bill, but you will end up paying over the total life of your borrowing. (you pay a lower rate of interest, but for longer). You may have decided to re---mortgage because your family needs more space and you calculate that it would be cheaper to raise money for an extension than to move house. (The extension will also add to the value of the property).

So you go to a mortgage broker-a good local firm if you know them and one who can cover the whole UK market for what you want. (as a check on what you are offered, investigate the mortgage market on the internet and look for direct-only deals). The broker's first job will be to check that you do not trigger any of the negative signals to finding a new mortgage.

NOT TOO SMALL

He will want to confirm that you have a good repayment history. He will also want to confirm that your existing loan is not too small (below £350,000) or has only a few years to run. If either of these applies-perhaps you left it too long to decide to re-mortgage- the costs of a re-mortgage will just be too large for the size of the deal.

Right at the start, you need to get the broker to take you through all the costs which will be involved (including the broker himself who will probably get a commission from the new lender as well as his fee from you). In particular, you need to be clear on which bills can be added to the loan and which you will have to pay out yourself.

YOUR EXISTING LENDER

So you are ready to begin what could prove to be your biggest financial saving in the squeeze years. Your first step should be to go to your existing lender and ask for a repayment quotation. Some lenders will allow you to borrow more as the value of your house increases. If you made overpayments on your mortgage in previous years, the lender may allow you to withdraw that money. If you challenge your lender for better deal and he responds in a positive manner, you may not need to re-mortgage. But there is a strong chance that your present lender will simply stay with the terms of the existing loan. That means he will charge a "redemption penalty" for quitting the deal. This must be specified in your original loan agreement (you should check) and could typically amount to six months' interest.

FEES BOTH WAYS

You know the type of mortgage deal you want, so you ask for a detailed quote from the new lender-or perhaps more then one lender. He will want to charge you a fee-often called an arrangement or administration fee- which makes you write down the fees you will have to pay. The two major items are those you have already come across, namely on redemption and on arrangement or acceptance.

Your property will have to be professionally valued for the new mortgage, raising another fee, and there will be the costs of your legal advice. Some lenders will pay your legal/valuation fees or give you a fixed amount and some will add the fees to the amount of your loan. You need a clear understanding of who pays what. At least, as this is a re-mortgage, you are spared the costs of moving house.

ASSUMPTIONS NEEDED

You now have a handle on the costs. You need to work out the benefits over two situations, say five years and 10 years, and this comparison will tell you whether or not a re-mortgage is good for you. If you have opted for a tracker mortgage, which is linked to base rate, you should also make further assumptions about future interest rates-high-end and low-end.

Everything looks positive, so you decide to go ahead. You or the broker make the application to the new lender, which nowadays is done over the internet or by telephone, rather than face-to-face. The valuation takes place, and the legal activity gets under way. After four to eight weeks, all the work should have been done. The lawyers arrange completion-you have re-mortgaged!

TWO AFTERTHOUGHTS

Afterthoughts in finance are not generally a good idea, but in this case there are two which are worth some reflection. One is insurance cover: you will have arranged insurance protection for your old mortgage, so you need to think whether that will be adequate for the new loan. If you re-mortgage because you got a better job, look at ASU (Accident, Sickness and Unemployment insurance).

Your second afterthought should be when you ought to decide to re-mortgage again. There is no limit to the number of times you can re--mortgage, and the test remains simple-will re-mortgaging make you better off? Mortgage finance is a fast-changing world, where the amounts involved are important for you.

So, you stay alert for the chance to make more money.

****

4

WORKING OUT THE HOLIDAY MONEY

You and your family deserve a holiday. You go online, book your flights and make the hotel reservations. Now, you need to think about holiday money.

You may be in for a surprise if you plan to travel beyond Europe and North America-maybe go to India or China or to see the Inca sites in Peru. You will not be able to buy these currencies in the UK. That is not because of some oddity in the foreign exchange market. Those governments want to keep control of their currencies, and will not have the value of their currencies traded in Europe or the US.

The pound in your pocket, like the dollar and the euro, is traded worldwide so that its value is fixed by the free-world markets. In China, the value of the yen is set by the central government, aiming, it is said, to keep its value down in order to expand their exports to Europe and North America.

CASH IN WHEN YOU LEAVE

When you travel to these countries, you have to buy local currency when you arrive at the airport. That means that you have to accept whatever rate of exchange is on offer. It also means that you need to cash in the local currency at the end of your holiday-and perhaps suffer another hit on the rate of exchange. When you leave, you will probably be offered a change into US dollars, as the currency which has greatest world-wide acceptance. Make sure you get the dollars, which you can keep or exchange when you are back in the UK.

You have to expect that ATMs and credit cards may be less widely used than back home and that banks will be less numerous- and may charge heavy commissions. Cash will be king, so you also carry a number of small-denomination dollar bills. Before you go, make sure that you have insurance cover for the currency you will be carrying-on your travel insurance, though you may be protected by your home contents policy.

RATES FLUCTUATE

If you go to Europe or North America, where the currencies are widely traded, you will want to take some money with you, (the more currencies are traded, the better deal you should get: less well-known currencies will cost you more). The first thing you notice is that exchange rates fluctuate, even from one day to the next, so you cannot be certain how much your £1,000 is going to get you.

There is no good answer to this problem: the best solution is to follow what the stock market calls pound averaging. If you are leaving on holiday in three months time, buy what you need in three equal instalments each one month apart. This will not guarantee that you get the cheapest exchange rate, but you should avoid the most expensive.

INTERNET MAY BE BEST

Which is the best way to buy foreign currency? Probably over the internet, though you need to check against the exchange specialists and travel agents in the high street-sometimes they will change their rates if you are offered a better deal on the net.

You may not be charged a commission, but remember that the seller makes his money on the "spread", which is the difference between his buying price and his selling price. He also makes money on the wholesale-retail difference: he buys in bulk at one price and parcels out at higher prices.

Some sellers will offer to buy back any currency which you bring home at the end of the holiday, and guarantee no dearer a rate than the one you paid. This represents a useful extra-so long as he is offering you a good rate of exchange on your money.

IT'S THE RATE THAT MATTERS

All that matters, when you buy foreign currency, is the rate of exchange. Some outlets will offer commission-free deals-but you should just concentrate on the rates you are quoted. All you need to know is the bottom line: how many dollars, euros or whatever you get for your pound sterling.

Where you live can affect how much you pay. The cheapest way to buy currency will probably be over the internet when you can go to the seller and collect in person (use cash for the best deal when you go and buy currency: you may be charged if you use credit or debit card.). If that is a problem-say if you live a long way from a currency outlet- currency sellers will probably deliver to your home or office, perhaps free of charge if you are buying £500 or £1,000 worth.

One of the more expensive ways to buy holiday money is to leave everything until the last moment and buy what you need at the airport when you leave.

TRAVELLERS' CHEQUES?

You need to take some local currency- if you are allowed to- when you go abroad, and most of your spend will be within the country itself. Until the 1960s and 1970s you would have taken travellers' cheques, which you can still do. You buy them from a bank or travel agent and you can choose any of the leading currencies-you take cheques in the currency of the country where you are going to travel, or in US dollars.

You sign the travellers' cheques when you buy. When you want to cash-in abroad you just counter-sign and present some ID. Travellers' cheques are numbered, so that if they are lost or stolen the bank can put on a stop and will send you a replacement. Travellers' cheques are a safe way to carry money.

Travellers' cheques will be accepted in big cities abroad, but elsewhere you may find that people are not keen to take them. They are used only by tourists, not the locals in their daily business, and there have been cases of forged travellers' cheques. When you want to cash them you will probably have to go to a local bank which you could find will hit you with hefty commission. One area where travellers' cheques still work easily is in the US where dollar-denominated cheques are widely accepted.

PLASTIC-BUT NOT QUITE THE SAME

Abroad, most people nowadays pay for their spend in the same way as they do in the UK- they use plastic. But not quite the same sort of plastic. When you read the small print of your credit card agreements (always a good thing to do, even if you do it only once) you will see that most UK cards charge you an extra 2.5-3% on foreign exchange transactions. This charge is made when the card company converts your holiday spend into sterling, so incurs a charge in order to make up your monthly bill.

SOME DON'T CHARGE

Not all card companies pass on this charge, so you need to take one of those- when this was written, they included Halifax and the Post Office, Nationwide (in Europe) and SAGA for the over 50s (remember to use one of those surcharge-free cards when you buy something over the internet which is priced in foreign currency).

But you will not use your credit card to draw cash when you are abroad- that is expensive. You could use your UK bank debit card, but that will probably also suffer from a 2.5-3% surcharge. There are two ways to sort this problem. One is to open a bank account where they do not make the surcharge (such as one of the companies in the previous paragraph) and use that debit card. That is cost-effective but rather cumbersome.

LOADED CARDS ARE NEATER

A neater solution is a loaded or prepaid card, as outlined in the chapter on credit cards. You can choose say a dollar or euro card and you load it buying the currency-so think pound averaging when you top up. (Exchange rates are usually average or better). You can use your loaded card abroad to draw cash at an ATM or, like a credit or debit card , to pay the bill in a shop or restaurant. No bank is involved when you apply for a loaded card (there is no credit element, you have just what you put onto the card) which simplifies the procedure. You can load someone else's card and someone else-say your employer-can load yours. A loaded card makes budgeting easier, and you can always top up if needed over the internet or telephone. Loaded cards are especially useful to get money to your son or daughter if they run out of cash when backpacking on some distant beach.

WORLDWIDE OPTION

You will not get interest from the money you keep on a loaded card and you need to check if there are any costs on opening and closing the card or when you top up. If you want a card you can use worldwide-say if you want to access dollars in Australia as well as US dollars and euros-expect to pay a surcharge on the transactions.

Using plastic is fine for normal holiday spend, but not if you are planning to send a sizeable amount of money abroad-say to pay when you rent or buy a villa. If you are looking at a spend of several thousand pounds, you need to think about some other options.

WHY CURRENCIES CHANGE

Your bank could help, but they may not be the cheapest route, in terms of charges to make the transfer and the exchange rate they get for you. Some discount brokers offer a currency service or you could use a specialist foreign exchange broker: many of the outlets which buy and sell currency in the high street can also help on bigger deals. You will need to shop around.

You make all these sensible moves but you are left with a big problem which you feel unable to solve-currencies move up and down, which impacts directly on the cost of your holiday. But no one seems to know why or when. Many clever people make their living by forecasting currency changes, but you need to look for the one key driver: currencies change because they chase yield.

CHASING YIELD

When the European Central Bank raised rates above the UK level, money moved to Europe where the yield was better-money would earn more, and the shift of currency made the euro rise and sterling fall. When the tsunami hit Japan, the yen fell because markets saw that industry would be disrupted and resources would have to be diverted into repairs and reconstruction- yields would fall.

The Australian dollar has been especially strong over recent months, partly because Australia's bank rate of 4.25% is one of the highest among leading countries-well above 0.5% in UK.

Like any financial market, the foreign exchange also looks ahead, generally around six to 12 months (any further gets too uncertain). Currency rates at any one time reflect what is happening today, combined with people's best guesses of the short- term future.

If a new leader is going to take over in China, will he stick to the previous plan- keep the currency down or let it float upwards? If there is going to be a general election in Australia, will the government change and how would that impact on interest rates and the dollar?

OUT OF THE BLUE

All this is made more difficult because some events just hit out of the blue- the tsunami in Japan, or a government's decision to call a general election. When you are going to buy holiday currency, adopting a policy like pound average has to be a sensible response. If you feel confident enough, you can always back your own judgment and buy when exchange rates move and the currency looks cheap!

If you plan to buy or sell a property abroad and deal with a large amount of currency, you should set up a forward contract. This means that you can fix today the sterling value of the dollars or euros which you will have to find (or receive) in six or twelve months. When the time comes, you may feel rather sad or very glad- but you will have had certainty. This after all, the kind of thing which farmers have been doing for the past hundreds of years.

****

5

LOVE YOUR BANK?

A bank account is just the most convenient way to handle the money you need everyday. The good news is that the risks, which looked so dangerous a few years ago, have been sorted. Your account now carries a government guarantee through the Financial Services Compensation Scheme which amounts to £85,000. The bad news is that there is little scope- with base rate at 0.5%- of making significant money from your bank. But you can avoid costs and save money by making your bank arrangements work for you. You start off with a basic bank account, which may still be enough for some people. Your wages can be paid in, you can pay in cheques or cash and set up direct debits. You will also get a cash card to draw money from ATMs. But you are not given a cheque book and you cannot get overdrawn. You should be able to monitor your account by telephone or over the internet. (remember that e-mails are not secure-so that banks will not accept e-mail instructions and you should not put confidential info in an e-mail)

DD/SO

The next stage up is a current account, where you do get a cheque book and you can set up an overdraft. (Though the bank

41

cheque is now an endangered species- people use a debit card over the telephone) You can also set up direct debits and standing orders, which is where you should pause. These take money from your account and you need to keep a close watch- they are just so easy to arrange.

- Direct Debit-bill payments direct from your account- the typical, way to pay credit card bills. Running the direct debit correctly is the bank's responsibility.
- Standing Order-regular set payments from your account to whoever you choose- this is how most people give their partner the weekly or monthly housekeeping.

THINK FEEDER

In the good old days, many banks paid interest on current accounts. Not now. So if you go into surplus, you need to set up a 'feeder' system. You open a savings account, which will pay some (though not much) interest, and the bank transfers anything over say £500 from your current account. If your account drops, the bank just reverses the process. This will not bring you serious amounts of money, but you will be making the best use of what is available.

The banks are starting to sort this problem by paying interest on accounts where you will be liable for a small monthly fee. You will be asked to pay in your monthly salary and you may also get cashback-varying on different types of spend which you will have to arrange by direct debit. It is a good sign that the banks are getting more flexible: whether it makes sense for you depends on the numbers. You have to sit down with a typical month's budget and do the math-remembering that you have to pay tax on bank interest.

But like most of us, your current account may go into the red especially just before payday. This is where you need to plan in order to save money. The first stage is where you go into the red occasionally, for a short time before you get paid.

Then you need to set up an overdraft, which allows your account to go negative (literally, draw more than you own). You will pay a significant rate of interest, plus setting-up and maybe annual charges. An overdraft represents the traditional bank facility, with the great benefit of flexibility-you just draw what you need.

TALK FIRST

If you go this route, it is vital that you stay within the overdraft figure which you have agreed. If you do not, it will cost you and start to give you a negative credit standing. If you think you will breach your agreed overdraft, always go and talk to the bank first. This applies even more when you go into the red without having arranged an overdraft. The bank may pay your cheque-and charge you a penalty for the unplanned borrowing. Alternatively, it will bounce it-'return to drawer'. Remember that banks, more than most people, dislike the unexpected.

Overdrafts are not cheap-early this year, the average rate came out just under 20%, only a little lower than during the crunch four years ago. But several banks offer attractive deals: a no-interest overdraft of £500 or £1,000 for people who pay in £1,000 a month (which means people who bank their salary).

When your overdraft occurs regularly and especially if it grows in size, the bank may suggest that you take a personal loan. This will be unsecured and for a fixed period of time. At present, expect to pay interest around 6-6.5% for a loan up to perhaps £15,000. A personal loan will make sense in terms of interest costs if you have to keep running an overdraft. The downside is its lack of flexibility-and the bank will expect you to follow the (usually monthly) repayment schedule.

A PAYDAY LOAN-AT 4,214 % ?

One day, sitting at home with your PC, you think how handy it would be if you had an extra £50 cash for just a week or two. What about a payday loan- what the bankers call a short-term small-principal advance?

You have a bank account, you get a regular paycheque, you are a UK resident and over 18, so you can go ahead- maybe even if your credit record is less than perfect. You could borrow say from £50 to £1,500 for a day or for up to a month. So you go online and ask for £50 for 30 days. The whole process is easy-no need to fax any documents and you make your application sitting at home.

AN OK HALF AN HOUR

You get approval in half an hour and in an hour or so the money is in your bank. When the 30 days are up, the amount of the loan plus the finance charges are taken automatically from your account. If you miss a repayment, you will be hit by a further charge, maybe leading to a blot on your credit history.

What did this cost you? Reality kicks in at this point, when you find out just how much interest you have been paying. One payday lender explains that its charges represent an annualised rate of 4,214%- which is 8,000 time the level of base rate (payday lenders have to show annual rates, though no borrower should ever dream of running payday loans for a year).

In your case, when you borrowed £50 for 30 days, you have to hand back £64.75. The charge for credit amounts to £14.75 on a one-month loan of £50. And that equals a yearly interest charge of 359% (three hundred and fifty nine per cent).

OUT NEXT PAYDAY

In some cases, the payday lender will take his money from your account on the next payday. When the charges are fixed per £50 borrowed, a shorter loan period will mean a higher interest rate. If you reckon a finance charge of between £10 and £14.75 per £50 borrowed, you will pay a representative annualised interest rate-as one payday lender explains-of 1,734% (one thousand seven hundred thirty-four per cent).

Under modern rules, payday lenders have to be upfront and transparent over their charges to customers. So you can be in no doubt if you take out a payday loan, that you will pay a rate of interest which is far beyond any normal scale. A representative rate 1,734% is more than three thousand times the level of base rate and around fifty times more than a credit card would charge.

A payday loan, i.e. a small cash loan for a short period, could sometimes be useful. But you need to explore all the other options-and maybe seek advice-before you think of paying interest rates at this level.

A PACKAGE ACCOUNT?

You and your bank are happy with your current account, so you are liable to be offered a package or premier account. The package account represents the next step up, offering say a small free overdraft and perhaps access to credit cards. There may be other freebies, such as mobile phone insurance. You should not have to pay for this sort of package deal, but the bank will probably ask you to ensure that £1.000 a month gets paid into your account. You guarantee that you will pay your salary into the bank.

OR CHOOSE PREMIER?

If you move to a premier account, you will be asked to pay-from £25 to £250 a month. For this, you will be offered a range of services, typically including travel insurance, breakdown cover, protection for your credit cards and access to airport lounges. At the top end of the charge scale, you will probably get a concierge service, where someone will arrange a holiday or book a table for you at a smart restaurant. You simply have to do a sum: do you want at least some of what is on offer and, if you do, could you get it more cheaply by shopping around? And always read the small print, e.g. to see if there is an age limit on travel insurance.

GOING JOINT

When you are living with a partner, you need to reflect how this impacts on the banking set-up. You could each keep a separate account-which probably works best when both of you are working and you just split the costs. The bank will assume that you are both responsible, so that if thing go pear-shaped it can look to each of you to make good any shortfall.

The other decision you have to make is whether the joint account needs both your signatures, or only one of you. If you hold joint investments, the dividends and interest should be paid into a joint account where either of you has the authority to sign.

BUT IF YOU SPLIT UP

That is also more practical for normal activities-if one of you travels, there could be a problem if you both have to sign. But remember: if the account is one where either of you can sign, and the relationship breaks down and you split up, then either one of you could empty the balance.

Banks are businesses, so that when interest rates are low-as they have been now for several years-they will stop paying interest on customers' current accounts, but keep up their charges to people who borrow. There is no mystery here: the banks make their profits from the difference between what they pay customers and what they charge borrowers. These profits are ploughed back into the banks' business or paid out as dividends to shareholders.

CREDIT UNIONS APPEAL

But suppose someone set up a financial service business which was controlled by its members and aimed just to break even rather than make a profit? The answer is a credit union, where the account-holders are the owners-a set-up which has attracted around a million savers and borrowers in the UK, and many more in the US and Europe. Credit unions across the world range from volunteer operations with a handful of members to sizable institutions owning several billion dollars of assets, with hundreds of thousands of members.

A credit union is a financial co-operative, where you can save as much or as little as you choose and expect to get an annual dividend. You can deposit at local shops, specified collection points or by direct debit from your bank account.

Many people like the idea that the owners are your neighbours and colleagues-membership here has more than doubled over the past 10 years. Just like a bank, all the money saved in a credit union is protected by the Financial Services Compensation Scheme.

LIMIT ON LOANS

Borrowing may be more expensive than from a bank, say 10-15%, but there is a legal maximum, set at 2% a month on the reducing balance. This equals an annual rate of 26.8%. Often, life insurance is built-in at no extra cost to pay off the loan in case of death. Some credit unions offer mortgages, cash ISAs and insurance products. Credit unions can typically help self-employed tradesmen finance their starter tools and equipment and there is now a proposal to make credit union accounts accessible at post offices. Their interest revenue tends to be small from typical low-amount short-term lending-which is partly why payday loan companies charge such high rates- so that part of the answer for credit unions probably lies in efficient processing.

6

PAY LESS TAX

Most of us lead simple lives, at least from a tax standpoint. That should mean that we all pay the correct amount of tax. But HMRC (Her Majesty's Revenue and Customs) make mistakes, sometimes on a massive scale. We, the taxpayers, change jobs, get married, have children all of which can affect the amount of tax we should pay. And all the evidence suggests we do not claim as much as we could.

So your first step towards paying less tax is simple: make sure that the taxman is up to date. He should know all about your age, address, marital status, job and so on. What the HMRC holds on your file may be out-of-date or just plain wrong. You need to keep them up-to-date and correct.

KEEP RECORDS

That also means you too need to keep records. You have a legal obligation to keep records for six years, and you will need this data if a dispute arises over what happened some time ago. You will also need these records if for some reason HMRC decides to launch an inquiry into your tax affairs.

There are times when you need to be extra vigilant, when things are more likely to go amiss. One is when your tax life changes-you get a new company car or decide to give one up in return for cash. Another time for vigilance is when HMRC itself changes and you find that your file is being handled in Penzance rather than Preston.

CODING MATTERS

You have to read, carefully, and keep what HMRC sends to you. A coding notice will arrive early in the year, which sets out the basis on which you will be taxed for the financial year which is about to start. Go through the coding notice and check out the taxman's forecasts-these form the basis on which you will be paying tax. All that will be summed up in a letter with numbers which will be sent to your employer's payroll department. If there is anything which looks suspect or which you do not understand, raise it.

Next you need to look at your family set-up from a tax standpoint. If you are single, this aspect is not that relevant- the possibilities start to arise when you are married or in a civil partnership or are in a non-formal relationship. In marriage or civil partnership, the key rule is simple: all income-producing assets should be held by whoever pays the lower tax rate, and all charitable donations should be made by whoever pays the higher tax rate.

GIFT AID TRIGGER

The rules on donations are simple. If you pay £100 to a charity, this is treated as net by HMRC. When you make a gift aid declaration, that triggers a £25 contribution from the taxman. This contribution was £28 until last April, as charities were paid an extra £3 to compensate for the fall in basic rate tax from 22% to 20%.

But this £25 contribution comes with a condition – that you, who made the donation, have paid at least £25 in tax. If you were a non-tax payer, HMRC would come after you to recoup the money which it had paid to the charity.

So non-taxpayers should not donate to charity-it is not tax-effective. But higher-rate taxpayers can claim the payment against their income on their tax returns. Someone paying 40% could reduce their tax bill by a further quarter of the gift, bringing the net cost down from £100 to £75.

SEIS/VCT/EIS?

Maybe you prefer a different approach- pay less tax by taking some risk. This points you towards making investments which bring tax benefits, where the government greatly widened the scope in last April's budget. Think Venture Capital Trusts, the Enterprise Scheme and the new Seed Enterprise Investment Scheme.

The SEIS which started to operate last April, aiming to encourage investment in start-ups, offer the most generous tax breaks. You get tax relief of 50% of the amount invested, irrespective of your own rate of tax, up to a maximum of £100,000 a year. SEIS also carries exemption from capital gains tax when you re-invest in another SEIS company during the same year. The SEIS shares themselves are free from CGT once you have held them for three years.

VCTs TO £15 MILLION

Venture Capital Trusts, which have been around for nearly 20 years, have had a mini-boom. When pension contributions were restricted, many people saw VCTs as an attractive long-term alternative. VCTs are listed companies which back British businesses worth up to £15 million (the limit was more than double last April).

When you buy a new issue of VCT shares, you get income tax relief up to 30%, on a maximum of £200,000 a year so long as you hold the shares for five years. Dividends and capital gains are tax-free. There are several established management groups which run VCTs-often divided into tech or generalist investment, investors on the Alternative Investment Market or VCTs with a predetermined fixed life.

Compared with traditional units, VCTs often ask for a high minimum investment and their management charges tend to be rather higher. It makes sense to invest through a discount broker.

EIS TO A MILLION

The Enterprise Investment Scheme, the third way to invest for a tax saving, also offers 30% income tax relief on shares in small, higher-risk unquoted companies. You have to hold for three years, but the maximum investment was doubled in the last budget, from £500,000 to £1 million.

SIMPLE STOCK TRANSFER

Income-producing assets are simple to move because there is no capital gains tax on transfers between spouses and civil partners. This means there is no tax come-back when you transfer shares and unit trusts, and CGT does not arise when you move cash. In order to make the transfer you simply have to complete a stock transfer form, which you can get from the company's registrar or from the manager of the unit trust-or just download the form over the internet.

A typical case is where the husband works full time while the wife stays at home to look after their young children. The objective is for the lower taxpayer to use up their tax-free allowance, which was raised to £8,105 last April and goes up again to £9,205 next year.

But the scope is even wider. It makes sense to transfer assets if one partner pays tax at 40% while the other pays 20%. This will also work between pensioners if one starts to lose age allowance-still useful despite the curbs in last April's budget-while the other pays basic rate tax.

OR GO JOINT?

Some people may hesitate about handing over all of their shares, unit trusts and bank deposits. There is a compromise, where you put the assets into joint names, so that you and your partner own them together (you use a stock transfer form, as with an outright handover).

Joint ownership usually means 50-50, so you will get half the tax benefit of a complete transfer. But you do not have to go 50-50- you can decide on any other division, so long as you tell the taxman.

HELP ON PROBATE

There is a side-benefit arising from the joint ownership of assets. When one of you dies, the jointly owned assets go to the surviving partner without the need for probate. If the assets were in single ownership, HMRC would want to be paid the inheritance tax before probate is granted and the assets can be transferred. In this way, joint ownership can provide financial help and avoid grief at a difficult time.

If you choose joint ownership, there is a further step you need to take. Open a joint bank account, which each of you can access, where the dividends and interest will be paid.

TAXMAN ATTACK

If the income continued to channel into the higher rate taxpayer's account (which no bank would allow anyone else to access) the taxman might have a basis to attack the deal. He could argue that the change to joint ownership was not real-and was no more than a simple ploy by the higher-rate payer to save tax. You definitely do not want them to start along that line of thought!

All these moves can help spouses or civil partners- but couples who are outside these two groups need to make some careful plans. Key point is that, to HMRC, a couple who are just partners have no tax position, they simple stand outside the system. At times, this can be useful: each member of a couple can keep a principal residence-potentially helpful tax-wise-while a couple who marry are allowed to own only one.

TRANSFERS CAN COST

But by the same logic any transfer of assets (half a holding or all of it) will attract capital gains tax. You can create a joint holding with your partner, but you will be restricted by the £10,600 CGT-free allowance plus any losses which you may have brought forward. Remember that when you make a gift, the taxman sees you making a sale at the prevailing market price.

And for all couples, whether formally linked together or not, a gift is a gift. When you transfer all or part of the shares and unit trusts which you own, they become the other person's property. So that if the relationship breaks down, you may have said goodbye to some of your assets (like if problems arise after you have set up a joint bank account which each of you can access).

TAX AT THE CLIFF-EDGE

One of the features to develop in the tax system over recent years has been the 'cliff-edge'. This means that if you receive income one day rather than the next, you pay a different rate of tax. Or if your income goes up-only because you worked harder- you find yourself paying a much higher rate of tax.

Two examples of a cliff-edge at work. Under the old rules, child benefit ended if one partner was paid £45,000 a year-while the two partners next door, who earned £40,000 a year each, were not affected. When 40% higher rate tax was raised to 50% for people earning £150,000, huge amounts of money-the Treasury estimates £2 billion was brought forward to the earlier year in order escape the extra 10% tax.

WHEN A DAY SAVES

This year, the expert's top-rate taxpayers had to rush again, this time in order to make their pension payments before 2013-14 when the rate comes down from 50% to 45%. A top- rate taxpayer would be £2,500 better off by making his year's pension contribution on April 5 next year rather than on April 6.

A cliff-edge can be a problem, or an opportunity. It will be a problem for about 300,000 people who will start to pay 40% higher rate tax when the threshold drops from £42,475 to £41,450. This is the exact opposite of the top taxpayer's position. On April 6 next year, someone earning £42,000 a year will get 40% marginal relief on his pension contribution. On April 5, his relief will be only 20%.

Here are some ways in which you might be able to benefit from the taxman's cliff-edge:

- If you are self-employed, work out carefully when income and expenditure arise in relation to the financial year and tax rates, and when you take a bonus or receive a dividend;
- If you are an employee, discuss bonus dates with your employer-one big insurance company pays bonuses on April 1 (just inside the tax year) but indicates that, when asked, it could pay on April 30 (just outside the tax year);

- When you make donations to charity, think whether you want to elect for them to be treated as if they had been made in the previous year-maybe if you moved from paying higher –rate tax to basic rate or from 50% to 45%;
- Think about transferring income –producing assets to your children, maybe to help pay for the costs of university. If a child's income reaches more than £100 a year from assets given by the parent, the taxman regards it as the parent's income-but when the child reaches age 18 they become an adult and all this changes! Rather than give the young student money out of your taxed income, you could give them assets on which they will pay tax at the standard national rate. If they have no other income, as from next April the first £9,205 will come tax-free. Seven years after you make your gift, that part of your estate will escape IHT.

You could pay 62%!

One of the sharpest cliff-edges comes when you start to approach a six-figure income. Your personal allowance starts to reduce once you reach £100,000 salary and disappears altogether by the time you get to £118,410. As you are losing your allowance and paying tax at the same time, you pay an eye-watering marginal rate-62% to be exact. People hoped that this anomaly would be corrected in last April's budget, but it remains unchanged.

Faced with this grim prospect, how do you keep your income down? Not the usual sort of problem! The immediate answer is to make pension contributions, which can be offset against tax up to £50,000 a year (see the pensions chapter). If you are content with your level of pension payments, think about another wide-ranging scheme to help you avoid paying 62%. Think salary sacrifice.

SACRIFICE SOME SALARY?

The theory is essentially simple: you give up some of your salary, on which you pay tax. In return you get a non-cash benefit which falls outside the tax net. If you draw a salary, you need to talk to your employer. If you are self-employed, you should speak to your accountant or direct to HMRC. The first step is to do the sums.

When you sacrifice salary, you pay less tax and NI. Your employer has a lower wage and pension bill and he also pays less NI. These savings, put together, create the pot which is used to pay your non-cash benefit. Some big employers have established salary sacrifice schemes, which were originally used mainly to add to employees' pension assets.

Now, the non-cash benefits have grown to include child care vouchers, extra holiday entitlement and car parking privileges. Some employers, who want to encourage people to cycle to work, have set up low-cost purchase deals with local suppliers.

TAX-FREE DEALS

Which non-cash benefit you choose has to depend on your own taste and what your employer can provide. But it is worth remembering that there is a range of deals which you could happily receive without starting any tax liability, such as :

- Financial loan on favourable terms up to £5,000;

- Free use of a computer;
- Use of a mobile phone, including rental;
- Medical check-ups for you and your family;
- Use of sports and leisure facilities;
- Pension advice and information.

****

7

INCOME OR CAPITAL

Hundreds of years ago, scientists tried to find the philosophers' stone which they believed would turn anything it touched into gold. For some people, today's philosophers' stone is something which would turn income into capital.

The appeal is simple: what you get as capital is taxed more lightly than whatever you receive as income.

Look at the numbers: for 2012-13, the first £10,600 of capital gains is completely free of tax. Above that, a basic rate taxpayer will be liable at 18% and a higher taxpayer at 28% (your gains are added to your income for the year). On income the basic rate kicks in at £8,105 for the under 65s and the higher rate starts to hit at £42,475. Personal allowances start to disappear at £100,000 and the top 50% rate begins (just for this year) at £150,000.

Next year, 2013-14, there will be no change to taxes on capital gains but the income tax picture will alter. Top rate taxpayers will be liable for 45% rather than 50% and the starting level for tax goes up to £9,205. Against this, pensioners suffer because their age allowances will be frozen. Many more taxpayers will face the 40% higher rate because the crossover point is reduced from £42,475 to £41 with 350-400,000 more people caught in the net.

TRADE-OFF FOR RISK

There is one snag. The taxman has also noticed why people prefer to receive capital rather than income, and he has drawn up elaborate rules to prevent us all saving huge amounts of tax in this way. But there is a way forward: accept the trade-off-an element of risk in return for a tax advantage.

You can see that the taxman would be bound to clamp down on any plan which simply and safely turned income into capital-the amount of income tax he claimed from taxpayers would go into free-fall. But if the income-into-capital plan is less than certain, because it contains an element of risk, then you can go ahead. The key is to accept a manageable degree of risk.

THINK ZDP

The traditional safe way to receive capital rather than income is to buy Zero-dividend preference shares. (ZDPs) These are issued by financial companies, generally investment trusts- you can buy them from the trust or through the stock market. If choice looks difficult, you can buy into a unit trust fund which holds this type of share. ZDPs pay no income: they are repaid at a pre-agreed price on a pre-agreed date.

You do the math, starting with what you paid and when. Then you factor in the re-payment price and date to give you a yield, which you can compare with unit trusts or term deposits with a bank. When the ZDP is paid, you will be showing a profit, on which you will be subject to Capital Gains Tax-not, repeat not, income tax. These shares offer a range of re-payment dates, so you can choose in order to meet your particular targets. ZDPs can be built into schemes to help pay the fees at university or private schools.

CHOICE TO 2018

ZDPs used to be popular, but hit problems at the end of the tech share boom a few years ago. Some trusts proved to be over-borrowed and many had been buying shares in each other. Cross-holdings have now been outlawed, and earlier this year there were around two dozen ZDPs available, offering redemption dates stretching out to 2018.

So how do you keep down risk? One answer is to stay with ZDPs which have been issued by one of the major financial groups-MandG, for example, have issued ZDP which runs to 2017. Before you buy, it is sensible to run a health check on the ZDP when you find one which meets your target date for re-payment.

CHECK BANK DEBT

Bank debt is a starting point- this was one of the problems for ZDPs a few years ago. There is no obvious reason for an investment trust to borrow heavily from the bank. If it does, the directors need to explain why. The next test has to be asset cover, which is simply the amount of assets available for the ZDP, which ranks ahead of the ordinary shares. You need to see asset cover of at least one, and preferably rather more.

A sophisticated version of the asset test is the 'hurdle rate'. This tells you how much the trust's assets will have to grow, in percent per year, in order to pay off the ZDP when re-payment falls due. A hurdle rate much above say 5% over a five-year life tells you that you will need good stock market performance if you want to be repaid in full.

WHEN NEGATIVE IS GOOD

Some ZDPs will show a negative hurdle rate. This means that the trust is already in a position to repay the shares and could even suffer some decline in the value of its assets yet still redeem the ZDP in full. A negative hurdle rate, say −5%, means that the trust's assets can fall 5% a year and still meet the payout at the end of the ZDPs life. That is about as comfortable as a ZDP shareholder can get. Zero-dividend preferences get close to the modern philosopher's stone-they produce no income, only capital and if you choose carefully the risk will be low. The problem is that ZDPs are a limited market and only a few trusts use this method of capital-raising (the maximum liability is much bigger than the amount initially raised). Specialists −and enthusiasts-can find zero shares and bonds more often on Wall Street and the eurodollar market. But for the average investor this represents a currency risk plus the extra costs of dealing.

STRUCTURES FROM BANKS

The banks reaction to the capital/income issue was to create 'structured' products −products which they had put together-which accepted an element of risk but which aimed to offer an appealing mix of overall return and tax efficiency. These products are inevitably complicated and a very good deal from bank to bank.

You will need a sizable investment, probably between £3,000 and £10,000. Do not necessarily buy direct. Think unit trust and use a discount broker (on the basis of execution-only) to get some cash back or a discount. You should get 1% or 5%, not a fortune but a useful £150 on an investment of £10,000. All the usual benefits of going to an adviser could also prove helpful-including someone to hassle if things get difficult.

STAY THE FULL TERM

Be prepared to commit your cash for the full term of the plan, typically around five or six years. You may only be able to access your money under penalty, or you may even be denied access altogether until the close of the plan. You might be able to put your scheme into an ISA or a SIPP. For anyone attracted by these schemes, the best way forward is to look at plans in detail. These schemes come in two broad types, income and growth. Here are two such, both designed by leading banks in the UK.

INCOME PLAN

- Your income comes at 6.25% a year, free of income tax. These payments represent a return of part of your original capital and are paid through a series of deposits-this is the tax benefit. For a 40% taxpayer, this represents a pre-tax return of 10.4%, which has a clear appeal especially in today's low-interest environment.

65

- As the income plan is linked to the stock market, you get small extra payments if the market is higher than when you started, reckoned on each anniversary. The extra is only 0.5% and is taxable-but, if it works, this means that a higher rate taxpayer will see his effective pre-tax return bumped up to an annual 10.9%.

- Downside-your capital will be at risk if the stock market does a nose-dive during the term of your income plan. You are covered for the first 50%: if share prices fall by no more than 50% your entire investment is returned when the plan terminates.

- So if the stock market falls by one third over the five years, you get all your money back- and you will have received five yearly payments of 6.25% equal to 31.25% of your investment. This 31.25% is subject to CGT: whether you have to pay tax will depend on the size of your investment and whether you make other gains (see the chapter on CGT).

- With the income plan, you lose out if the stock market falls by more than 50% and does not recover at least to where it started. If that happens, you do not get all your money back at the end of the plan-you suffer a 1% cut for every 1% fall in the stock market average. If share prices collapse at the crucial time, you could lose part of your capital. You did not have a safety net which protected your initial investment-though you will have received a useful level of income.

GROWTH PLAN

A typical growth plan will aim to offer you the best of both worlds-a benefit if share prices rise, but a safety net if stock markets go into severe decline at specified times. In return, you will not get any interest or dividends from the capital you invest.

- You will probably find an interim "kick out" option, which is designed to cope when everything goes faster than expected. If the stock market has say 10% after only three years into life of the plan, then you get all your investment back plus a gain of 35%. This gain is subject to CGT, but remember that you will not have received any interest or dividends.
- You may be given the option to continue the plan after kick-out, but you will not benefit from any further rise in the share prices. If there is no kick-out, you get your money back when the plan matures plus the rise in the stock market-if there is any!
- If the stock market is lower at the end of the plan than the beginning, you simply get money back. You will have a loss thanks to inflation, but your original cash investment is safe-which is why these schemes are often advertised as 'protected plans'. In one sense, you cannot lose.

Any share-based plan of this kind, income or growth, is inevitably rather inflexible-which you choose must depend on your own requirements, and how well you do depends on how the stock market is performing on certain specific dates fixed well in advance. This is why a typical growth plan will base its result on an average over the previous 12 months, rather than on one specific date. But you still have to face a loss of flexibility: you have to tie up your cash and if you held your own investments, you could take advantage of a sudden share price upsurge to seize a handy profit.

OPTIMIST OR PESSIMIST?

Your decision whether to buy into this sort of scheme, income or growth, will depend on how you see the stock market in the years ahead and on your appetite for risk-how important is a safety key? No one expects you to make a share price forecast, but you need to judge whether you feel like an optimist or a pessimist for the next five years.

Under the income plan, moderate pessimism will not cost you, as you get your money back even if the market falls 50%. Under a protected growth plan, you are cushioned even if share prices go into serious decline.

CHECK STATUS

There is one final check to be made if you decide to invest. You need to form a view of the financial status of the sponsoring business and of the other banks and financial businesses which will probably be involved (what bankers call the 'counter-parties'). You can check with one of the rating agencies, such as Standard & Poor, Fitch or Moody's.

Structured plans, put together by the sponsoring banks, often involve a chain of financial businesses-and like any chain, they will be as strong as their weakest link.

****

8

MONEY FROM YOUR HOUSE-RENT A ROOM

The squeeze is hurting. You need more capital and bigger income. So you look at your assets-the biggest is the house where you live. How can you set it to work?

If you have a spare room or a loft, you could be sitting on a tax free earner. Under the official Rent a Room scheme you can take in a lodger and you do not pay any tax on the rent up to £4,250 a year. That is worth £5,300 if you pay tax at standard rate and over £7, 000 if you pay tax at 40%

IN YOUR MAIN HOME-FURNISHED

There are two key features of Rent a Room. The room you let must be furnished and it has to be in your main home, where you and your family live for most of the time. You do not have to be the owner and you yourself may be renting. Nor does it have to be property which you choose as your main residence for capital gains tax-useful when better-off parents buy their son or daughter a house at university. A lodger means someone who pays to live in your home.

JOIN OR NOT TO JOIN?

Before you probe further into the do's and don'ts" you need to check out the numbers. The £4,250 comes free of tax, but you cannot offset expenses, such as wear and tear, insurance, heating etc. You have a choice:

- Route 1 is where you do not join the Rent a Room scheme-you take the rent, offset expenses and pay tax on the difference;
- Route 2 is where you join the scheme, do not account to the Revenue for expenses, and pay tax on any income you receive over £4,250 a year.

WORK OUT THE NUMBERS

If your expenses come in relatively high, perhaps because you could not let the room through the year, then you will probably follow Route 1 and not join the scheme. If expenses are low, and you have a steady income, you will probably join- the numbers will also depend on where you live in the UK. You have to work out which route leaves you better off.

We are talking a tax break here, so the taxman has set up a small minefield of rules and regulations. It is probably easier to start with the negatives. Rent a Room was set up 20 years ago to boost the stock of residential accommodation, so you cannot use the scheme if you let to a business for offices or storage (rent a Room will still work if your lodger does some business work at home in the evening or at weekends).

INDIVIDUALS ONLY

Nor will the scheme apply if your home has been converted into separate flats which you let out, though it will still work if you live in a caravan or on a houseboat. Rent a Room applies to individuals, not to companies or partnerships.

Thankfully, there are also important positives. You can join the scheme if you run a bed and breakfast or a guest house, so long as it is your main residence. If you provide meals, these count towards the £4,250 limit. If you get more than that you will have to pay tax-even if the amount of the rent itself is less.

ALLOWANCE SHARED

It is even possible for you and your partner each to operate a Rent a Room scheme, if your home is big enough, the £4,250 is shared between you. You each get a half-allowance of £2,125. Apart from tax, there are some practical issues to solve if you are attracted by the prospect of useful net income. You will need to check whether you need to get consent from the local authority. You will almost certainly have to talk to the lender if you are buying your house on a mortgage. If you are renting your home, you need to confirm that the lease allows you to take in a lodger. You will definitely have to contact your insurance company to make sure that you still have cover on the building and contents. And when you take in a lodger, you should do some basic checking on his credit and legal history-and you should always operate with a written agreement.

9

EQUITY FROM YOUR HOUSE

The one way to get significant money from your house is to tap into the equity you own. This amounts to the value of your house, less any mortgage or any other debts which you may still be outstanding. So your first step is to get some idea of what your house is worth. It is too soon to pay for a formal valuation, but talking to a couple of local estate agents should give you a reliable 'armchair valuation'. Be aware how house prices on average have performed-they more than doubled in the 10 years from 1996 to2006, went into reverse during the credit crunch and have now recovered to where they stood about two years before the peak.

That means that if you bought your house over the last five to seven years, then you are not likely to be showing much equity. But remember that these are average values and different regions have performed very differently-prices in London and the south east have done better than average.

EXTENSIONS COST
So how do you tap into the equity in your house? If you are in your 30s or 40s, with an existing mortgage, the answer is to re-

mortgage (see the earlier chapter). Some people have been extending their mortgages, attracted by the current low level of interest rates. The independent experts are against mortgage extension, partly because the next shift in interest rates will be upwards and partly because you end up paying so much extra interest-one of them reckoned that extending from 25 years to 40 would double your interest bill.

But suppose that you are in your 50s or 60s and want to tap into your house's equity? You need to know that there has been a massive shift in the mortgage market-in your favour! Not so long ago, banks and building societies used to insist that loans did not extend beyond 65 or70. All that has changed. Many now go to 75 or later and some have even dropped all age limits. Two of the largest building societies now allow borrowers to be up to 85 at the end of the loan term.

PAYING INTEREST AT 100!

What is probably the largest lender in the mortgage market has produced an intriguing product aimed at borrowers over age 65-no maximum age is specified. This is an interest-only mortgage, where the only requirement is that you pay interest every month. The term of the loan is set at a maximum of 40 years, so that you could-in theory-still be paying interest when you reach the ripe old age of 100 and beyond!

When the borrower dies, the property is sold and the mortgage is paid off. There are no restrictions on how you use the money which you have borrowed. One appealing feature of this scheme is that you can re-mortgage if you have a repayment mortgage with another lender, where you will be making payments on both interest and capital each month. That way, you give up the obligation to make any repayments on the loan and benefit from a lower-rate, interest-only monthly payment. This is getting close to equity release, where one of the key features is that you do not have to make any loan repayments-all that is done after your death from the sale of your house.

EQUITY RELEASE-INTEREST ROLLS UP

But there is one important difference between this mortgage for potential 100 years olds and equity release. This is an interest-only mortgage, so you have an obligation to pay monthly interest. Under equity release, you have no interest to pay-those costs are rolled up and added to the loan when it finally comes to be repaid. You need to pause at this point, because the difference will be highly significant for some people. Most people's income falls when they retire, so you need to think before committing a part to mortgage interest. For many borrowers, one of the main objects of equity in their home is to boost their retirement income-so this mortgage works the other way. And most people, when they retire, just want to stop having to worry about a mortgage.

So you have now decided just what you want: a lifetime mortgage, where the loan is paid off by selling your property when you die and where all the interest is rolled up and paid for, along with the capital you owe, when you die. You have just defined equity release.

OR YOU DOWNSIZE
Before you decide to go there, you need to think about downsizing-selling your existing house and moving to somewhere

75

smaller. Many people look hard at downsizing when the children go to university or move out altogether. All the surveys suggest that most people do not wish to downsize despite the financial advantages-you sell your house, keeping your profit free of tax (no CGT on the gain from selling your principal residence) and you have to use only part of the money to buy the downsize flat or country cottage.

But the move will cost you (mainly stamp duty on the new place) and there will be significant hassle factor. Many people are not keen to change location-leaving the house they have lived in, giving up a pleasant and safe neighbourhood, the GP they know, etc. But you should go through the financial numbers, which can be appealing.

AGE THE KEY

Your age is the key issue here. If you are under 55-60, you should take out a new mortgage or re-mortgage. If you are older, you opt for an interest-only mortgage or, if you do not want to pay monthly interest, you choose equity release (ER).

ER gives you between 20% and 40% of the value of your house, paid as a lump sum or income if you choose. Lenders typically require a minimum value of £75,000 on a house-it may be more difficult to get equity release if you live in Scotland or Northern Ireland.

YOU STAY THE OWNER

Most ER deals come as a lifetime mortgage. On a £250,000 house you could get £50,000 which will be paid when you die or go permanently into care, and you continue to own your house. You have no interest bills to pay-that is all rolled up, to be paid off with the loan capital.

You will find that the interest rate is higher than on a conventional mortgage and it will probably be fixed for the life of your loan. If you still have a mortgage outstanding, that will be wiped out under the new loan. You may come across SHIP-Safe Home Income Plans-which is a group of major ER lenders who agree rules for dealing with customers.

HOME REVERSION OPTION

Some people worry about interest rolling up over the years-especially as we are all living longer. There are two ways round this question. One is for you to pay the cash interest, turning equity release into an interest-only mortgage, and possibly with the option to switch to rolled-up interest in later years. Or you can opt for home reversion, which is the alternative type of ER.

Under home reversion, you sell a part of your house-say 20% or up to 100% if you choose. Minimum age will be rather higher than for a lifetime mortgage, though the discount to market value will be similar (the lender will tell you he may have to wait a long time for his money). You may be able to start with 20%, then raise the percentage and get more cash over the years. You give up ownership of your house and become a tenant for life (or until you go into care) for a nominal rent, with obligations for maintenance and insurance.

Under home reversion, there is no interest to roll up: when the house is sold the lender takes his 20% or whatever of the proceeds. With this route, you can be certain to leave part of the value of your house to the family-whatever that turns out to be worth. You also need to think about insurance protection-there will be a financial cost if you die or go into care shortly after completing a home reversion plan.

WHAT WILL IT WILL COST?

None of this comes free, nor can it be done quickly-allow six to eight weeks for a lifetime mortgage and maybe four weeks more for home reversion. The sequence is straightforward: you go for advice, appoint a solicitor and decide on a particular lender. The lender arranges a valuation of your house, then sends an offer to your solicitor. You accept and your solicitor hands you the money, less his own fee and after paying off any mortgage you still have outstanding. You need to look at the costs:

- Valuation. Essential for a lifetime mortgage or home reversion, say £250 for a £250,000 house, which you pay upfront.

- Solicitor. The lender will insist you appoint your own solicitor, who will probably charge around £500-which will come off the amount you receive.

- Lender. Will probably want an arrangement fee, likely to be £500-£700 which can be added to your loan.

- Advice. Unless you felt confident enough to approach a lender direct, your adviser will want a fee for finding the lender-say 1-2% of the amount you raise.

It is always worth checking around, either yourself or through an adviser. When this was written, one of the major lenders was offering £750 cashback on completion plus a free valuation on properties up to £500,000.

MORE OVER THE YEARS

The lifetime mortgage is simple, and you may be able to increase it over the years as house prices move up. You can set up a deal to drawdown your loan in stages if that suits you-which will save on your interest bill. Under home reversion, you are selling off part of your house. So what are the points you have to look for?

The first is to talk to your family, because the house will be sold when you die or go into care, and there will be a sizeable debt to pay off. You need to work out compound interest, which is good for investors but stiff for borrowers. If you take a £50,000 loan at say 6%, you will owe £90,000 at the end of 10 years.

NEGATIVE EQUITY GUARANTEE

The longer you live, the bigger the interest bill will grow though you will get a 'no negative equity' guarantee. Even if you live to a very ripe old age, so that the bill mounts up, your heirs will be free from any liability when you die. If the loan plus interest amounts to more than the value of the house, the lender takes the hit. Benefits from the state or local authority may become an issue under ER. They see you getting a lump of cash or a useful boost to your income, which could affect what you receive in tax credits or council tax relief. You need to check this out before you go very far.

LONG TERM DECISION

You should also accept with either type of ER, lifetime mortgage or home reversion, that you are taking a long-term decision. It may be possible to end your scheme after a few years if your situation changes, but redemption will be complex and it will cost. Reversing home reversion, from the way it is arranged, will not be simple.

If you have a lifetime mortgage the lender has to quote, in his annual statement to you, what it would cost if you wanted to redeem before you die or go into care. He will want to recoup the profits he expected if you had stayed with the plan, so the cost could be significant. You have some consolation, that all ER now comes under the Financial Services Authority, so that you will be able to access the ombudsman service if you hit major difficulties.

****

10

SAVING TAX-FREE

The Individual Savings Account, always called ISA, is a must for higher-rate and top-rate taxpayers. An ISA is a wrapper-not an investment in itself-which will protect shares, unit trusts and cash from any further tax.

How much you can put into an ISA is settled for every tax year, and has been fixed at £11,280 for 2012-13. Half of this, or £5,640, can be invested in cash, with the rest in shares and unit trusts-or the ISA can be invested 100% in shares. You have to invest during the tax year-from April one year to 5 April the next-because the annual allowance does not carry over. Use it or lose it!

NO JOINT ISAs

An ISA always has to be your investment, because the official rules do not allow a joint ISA. You and your partner can have one each and you can each invest as much as you choose up to the maximum allowed. The rules simply state that you have to be a UK resident and aged over 18 (a children's ISA, THE Junior ISA, was introduced last year with different rules; see later in this chapter)

The procedures for buying and selling an ISA are simple. You can go into the high street branch or building society, but most people invest by telephone or online. All you need is your National Insurance number and a debit card-and enough in the account to cover the amount you invest.

DON'T TELL THE TAXMAN

You do not have to tell the taxman about your ISA, nor about any income you receive or the profit you make when you sell your investment. ISAs simply operate outside the tax system. On this basis, there is no limit to the amount you can hold in ISAs. If you had invested the maximum each year since ISAs were set up in 1999, you would have a tax-free nest egg which would have cost you just over £100,000.

ISAs have clear appeal for 40% and 50% taxpayers, but for standard rate taxpayers the situation is more complex. For standard rate taxpayers, there is no benefit on the dividends you get from shares which are held in an ISA. Capital gains will come tax-free, but we can all make £10,600 of tax-free gains in any year. It still makes sense for standard-rate taxpayers to keep their cash assets and bond unit trust in an ISA and avoid the 20% which would normally go to the taxman.

TAX YOU CAN'T GET BACK

All this complication arose because the rules were changed in 2004, so that ISA holders can no longer claim back the 10% tax which companies withhold when they pay out share dividends. (pension funds and non-taxpayers are in the same boat). Following that change, it is no longer strictly correct to call ISAs 'tax-free'. There is no further tax to pay on the dividends you receive.

Bonds are treated differently from shares: If you hold bonds in an ISA, you can claim back the 20% tax which has to be deducted from interest payments. If you opt for a bond unit trust, the managers can still reclaim the tax provided that at least 60% of the fund is invested in bonds. For this reason, ISAs make an especially suitable home for fixed interest unit trusts (some of the major bond funds arrange an 80-20 split between bonds and shares, to give a growth kicker).

USE A DICOUNT BROKER

When you buy share or bond unit trusts, you should use a discount broker-ISA discounts can be especially attractive. The discount broker will use one of the investment 'platforms' such as Cofunds or Fidelity or they may run their own. You just need to check that there is no further platform charge to hold the particular funds you have selected.

People who use ISAs tend to follow one of three investment strategies:

- Make maximum use of the cash allowance, set at £5,640 for the current tax year and invest the rest in fixed-interest unit trusts-gilt-edged or bonds.
- Ignore the cash allowance and use all the £11,280 to invest in bonds and tracker unit trusts. (You can put shares into an ISA, probably using a broker, but most people choose unit trusts)

- Compromise by splitting your ISA 60-40 or 70-30 between shares and cash. Remember that you can invest in US or European shares-not just the UK-or the related unit trusts.

THINK 'BED AND ISA'

Many people use cash to set up their ISA, but it is also easy to switch an existing investment into an ISA, so your dividends or interest go from being taxable to tax-free. This is known as 'bed and ISA' because the taxman insists that your existing shares or unit trusts cannot just be moved across-they have to be sold and then bought within the ISA. You are liable to Capital Gains Tax if you make a profit, though the £11,280 ISA celling means this will probably fall within your annual tax-free limit on gains, which is fixed at £10,600 for 2012-13. If you make a loss, you can use that to offset other gains or carry the loss forward to future years.

In the old days, you could establish a loss for CGT by selling shares or unit trusts and immediately buying them back, which was known as 'bed and breakfast'. The Treasury then ruled that you had to wait at least 30 days before doing the buyback-this limited bed and breakfast deals because in a month the market could move against you. But by using an ISA you can sell, establish your CGT loss then buy back immediately through the ISA and avoid the market risk. Remember 'bed and ISA'- it could come in useful.

YOU CAN DRIP-FEED

When you decide to use cash to buy shares or bond unit trusts, most providers will allow you drip-feed your investment into the

ISA over the course of the financial year. This is what the stock market calls pound-averaging, which makes a lot of sense when share and bond prices are volatile.

So you set up your ISA and happily collect your income with no more tax to pay. But you want to change your investments-maybe your circumstances have altered, maybe you are not happy with the fund performance (you will have to change investments to keep up with the best deals on cash). If you want to make a withdrawal from an ISA, the first test has to be the official rules. These do not limit what you take out, but they do control what you can put in.

The £11,280 which is in force this year sets the maximum you can put into an ISA during 2012-13. If you have already invested the maximum and withdraw £2,000 you cannot put any more into an ISA until April 6 next year. In the same way, if you have put £10,000 into your ISA and you withdraw £3,000, you can only invest another £1,280 in an ISA (you have used £10,000 out of your £11,280 allowance-your withdrawal is ignored). Under the official rules, withdrawals are easy but access to an ISA is strictly limited.

DO NOT CASH IN

You may not want to withdraw any funds-you may wish simply to move your ISA to another group, maybe because you are attracted by a fund operated by the new manager. The golden rule, which arises from the official regulations, is that you do not cash in your investment, because you have no automatic right to re-invest. In order to keep the tax-free status on your investment, you have to approach the new manager and get him to make the transfer. You have to stay out of the transfer process, or risk losing your ISA allowance. There are some limits on your freedom to change ISAs. A current year cash ISA can be moved to another cash ISA or to a share ISA. A current year share ISA can only be moved to another share ISA-and you are not allowed to split current year ISAs, and you can split your investment. The same applies to a share ISA- except that you cannot move any of it into a cash ISA.

TRANSFER MAY COST

Transferring or withdrawing ISA assets may raise issues with the managers which you need to resolve, as far as you can, before you first invest. You may want to move to another manager, but you could find that 'transfers' in are not accepted. In that case, the manager will only take new investment in cash- and maybe only from new customers. Your next issue may come with the manager you want to leave.

Some will transfer investments, but others will only transfer cash and will insist on liquidating your investment. The important factor to check when you begin is whether the manager will charge an exit fee if you want to transfer. One of the largest ISA managers will charge £30 on each holding if you want to transfer out.

ISAs FOR JUNIOR

ISAs have become popular because their tax free status means that dividends and interest can compound so much faster than in the taxable world. This is ideal for long-term investment- and since last year, ISAs for the first time are open to children who do not have a Child Trust Fund. The tax benefits are the same as an adult ISA (no capital gains tax, no further tax on income) but the other rules are different:

- Allowance fixed at £3,600 per child per tax year-but will rise in line with inflation from 2013;
- No withdrawals allowed until the child reaches 18, though they can take responsibility for the account from age 16; at 18 the account automatically converts into an adult ISA and the child has full access;
- Children will be limited to one cash ISA and one stocks and shares ISA at any time. You cannot invest each year's allowance with different ISA suppliers-as you can with the grown-up version

This timing makes a junior ISA a big potential help towards paying for university or helping to build the deposit for a first-time house purchase. Never forget the power of compound interest: if you put in no more than the basic £3,600 and this grows at 6% a year (the FSA assumption for share prices) lucky junior will have a £10,300 asset by the time he or she reaches age 18.

If you look back over the last 18 years, the best-performing unit trusts-natural resources or US-linked- did about double that!

ANYONE CAN HELP

The way a junior ISA works is that the parent opens the account and manages it. Anyone can then contribute up to the annual limit- grandparents, family or friends. Just remember that contributions cannot be returned. They belong to the child ISA holder, and they stay out of reach until the child turns 18.

Managers will probably accept a minimum lump sum of £500 or £50 a month. Any child can have a junior ISA so long as they are resident in the UK and did not qualify for a Child Trust Fund as created by the previous Labour government. (unlike the Child Trust Fund, there is no government contribution towards a junior ISA). This points to two large groups who are eligible:

(1) Children under 18 who were born before August 2002, and
(2) Children born since January 2011.

OR BUY PREMIUM BONDS?

All this sounds great, you say, but why not just buy tax-free premium bonds-now held by a third of the entire UK population? The short answer is that Premium Bonds are not an investment, but a lottery where the odds are stacked in favour of the Treasury. Anyone can buy up to £30,000 worth of Premium Bonds and then rank for a prize at the monthly draw. The size of the draw is fixed by the Treasury who pay an annual interest rate of 1.5%. There are well over a million prizes every month, ranging from £25 to the single top prize of £1 million. Unlike the National Lottery, you do not lose your capital which rolls over to the next draw- the money you put in is safe, even if you do not win a prize.

EYE-WATERING ODDS
In any month, the chances of winning a prize are 24,000 to one. The chances of becoming an overnight millionaire are an eye-

watering 43,000 million to one. If you put the maximum £30,000 into Premium Bonds, the chances are that you will win around 15 prizes during a year, almost all £25 each. On this basis, you will earn around 1% tax-free on your money. All this is based on average luck (as opposed to yours or mine) which underlines the key feature of Premium Bonds-there are no guarantees.

BUY AND FORGET

Premium Bonds have appeal for two different sets of people. Any of us could buy the minimum £100 worth, put the certificate in a safe place and then forget about it. Over the years either nothing happens or you get a nice surprise. At the other extreme, a top-rate taxpayer who is cash-rich could buy the maximum £30,000 Premium Bonds once he has used up his ISA allowance. He could easily do better in terms of yield but he might regard the chance of a prize as worth something. Between these two extremes, the odds favour the Treasury.

****

11

YOU NEED A CUSHION

You have organised your basic financial structure-cash to deal with short-term issues, you have moved into tax-free ISAs and you have a pension set-up. You feel you now need a cushion, somewhere you can squirrel away any extra cash which will give you rising income over the years and grow into a significant asset by the time you come to retire.

Where do you find this cushion?

The traditional answer was to buy shares, where you would take a five year view and expect rising dividends and capital values. For many people, unit trusts replaced shares because individual companies could prove risky and unit trusts offer liquidity, i.e. they are easy to buy and sell. Unit trusts also enable you to avoid the deadly investment trap of putting all your eggs in one basket.

LOSS AFTER 10 YEARS

Sadly, this traditional answer has not looked so good over the past 10 years or so. The end of the dot-com boom was followed by the credit crunch-so that someone who bought an average parcel of shares around the year 2000 will still be showing a loss on his investment. You could look elsewhere-if you are dealing in millions. For the average saver/investor there is effectively no option apart from shares, cash and unit trusts. Property represents an option for some people (a buy-to-let or a holiday home) but it can be easier to buy than sell and you face putting a lot of your net worth into one particular asset. The seriously wealthy buy commodities, expensive works of art, large pieces of real estate or join together to organise private equity businesses.

YOUR AGE MATTERS

In today's squeeze, you are in a box. The way out has still to be unit trusts-keeping your costs to the bare minimum. Just before you start, two issues need to be resolved. The first is your age: the older you are, the closer you are to retirement and the more you need to keep in fixed interest funds.

People used to say that age, in years, had to equal the percentage you kept in fixed-interest bond funds. At age 30, you would hold 70% in equity-based unit trusts. At age 50, now 10 years away from retirement, your assets would be split equally between equity and bond funds. This is a simple formula, but it solves the 'lifestyle' issue-where advisers such as insurance companies gradually move you from shares into fixed interest as the years go by.

HOW RISKY?

The second issue you have to resolve is risk- how much can you face? You reduce risk by not putting all your eggs in one basket and by actively spreading your assets. Some people happily accept a high level of risk, say a situation where you double your money or lose it. You should work out a 'worst case' situation just in case everything goes pear-shape. There is no right answer here, but what you (and your family and friends) find comfortable. You should check that your risk-taking is paying off in terms of better performance-there is no point in running risks if, in the end, you do little or no better than the man who plays it safe.

YOU NEED A BROKER

When people think equity, most of them think about buying shares. The big difference between buying shares and unit trusts is-again-risk. You are investing in one particular company, which can grow like Apple or hit a short-term problem like BP. To buy and sell shares you have to go to a stockbroker who will charge (you need to check around on brokerage costs: internet is cheaper than telephone) but may also give you investment ideas and provide you with financial data.

One new, though controversial, compromise is the Exchange Traded Fund. An ETF, which is listed on the stock exchange, aims to track a particular index or asset. The biggest ETF tracks Wall Street, and you can buy ETFs which follow stock markets in Korea or Taiwan. You can also buy ETFs which follow gold, oil or grain prices. Charges are low, but you have to pay brokerage costs as they are listed (this could become a significant item if you are a regular buyer or seller).

ETF ISSUE

Not everyone is enthusiastic about ETFs. Some of the specialised ETFs have hit liquidity problems-at times you may find it difficult to buy and sell. Leveraged ETFs hit problems in volatile markets (their ability to borrow could be an advantage over unit trusts) and some commodity-centred ETFs performed less impressively than the commodities themselves. Instead of holding physical oil, gold or grain they would buy forward contracts which become a separate market (physical ETFs which hold the underlying assets are contrasted with synthetic ETFs which gain their exposure by means of contracts with banks).

In the UK-Wall Street tastes are somewhat different-ETFs remain a specialist interest, while most investors choose among the several thousand unit trusts which are now available. Two issues arise-which sort of unit trust do you buy, and just how do you buy them?

BONDS OR SHARES?

BONDS The money which you put into bonds should be channelled through a unit trust. You can buy a bond issued by a company but that is risky and may not be easy to trade. Your other issue is whether to buy high yield or investment grade. The high yield bond is riskier, which the yield is meant to compensate. An investment grade bond fund will yield less, but will be safe. A compromise is to have some of each.

SHARES You have the world to choose from-almost literally. One attractive sector is UK Equity Income: ordinary shares, often in large companies, which give an above-average dividend yield. The theory is that you get an income approaching bond fund rates, but you have the growth prospects of ordinary shares. And the above-average yield should provide some protection if markets go into reverse.

THE PRO CHOICE

Choosing investments is a book in itself, but try one scenario. Here is the range of choices revealed earlier this year by half a dozen professional fund managers as regards their own ISA portfolios:

- Bonds
- UK Equity income
- Energy sector world-wide
- Emerging markets-Asia, India and through UK-based 'umbrella' funds.

But there is a key element missing here-costs. The FSA suggests that you think of growth from shares or unit trusts averaging about 6% a year. That is much better than in the recent past, and close to the average if you go back over the last fifty to a hundred years. What do you have to pay to get 6%?

The short answer is that unit trusts will charge you around 5% when you initially invest and then about 1.5% a year to manage your money. This means that all of your first year's growth will be eaten up by charges-and from then onwards the manager will take one quarter of the trust's yearly growth.

DISCOUNT BROKER FIRST

That represents a heavy cost which you need to reduce. Your first step is to go to a discount broker. In return for your business he will drop all or most of the initial charge and may also pay you an annual loyalty bonus. The discount broker will not give you advice-he operates on an 'execution-only' basis-though he may give you financial data to help you choose your investments.

He can work this way because the fund manager gives him a piece of the yearly management charge-known as his 'trail commission' which he receives so long as you stay invested. The discount broker may get 0.5% out of the 1.5% which the manager charges and he can afford to pay you say 0.15% as an annual bonus. He will use an 'investment platform'- a kind of wholesale warehouse for shares and unit trusts- to organise the administration, or he may set up his own platform if he is big enough.

FEE FOR COMMISSION

There are around a dozen or more leading discount brokers and you have to check what they have to offer, both in terms of cash and providing research material, if you want that. When this was written, the best deal available was where the broker charges you a relatively small flat fee and you get to keep all of the initial commission and all the trail commission.

But this happy set-up may be in for a change, as the FSA and other authorities are taking a hard look at trail commission. In theory, the manager pays trail commission so that the broker can provide you, his client, with on-going help and advice. In reality, you may be sent ideas and share suggestions-or you may hear only occasionally from the broker, who is busy collecting his trail commission.

Most, but not all, managers pay trail commission to brokers. You need to be alert to this, because a discount broker who does not receive any trail commission may add an annual charge to your investments by way of compensation.

THINK TRACKER

Bottom line: you need to keep investment costs to a minimum and still stand to benefit from rising share and unit trust prices. The answer has to be: the tracker. This is a unit trust which tracks, i.e. it replicates, a particular stock market index- the London top 100, Wall Street and many others. Trackers show two key features:

Costs are low-you can buy a tracker from a leading bank for no initial charge and a management charge of 0.25% a year.

Trackers perform better than most managed funds.

You can afford to buy a tracker direct from the manager; the charges are so low that there is no space for discount brokers. The tracker's charges are so low because they just hold the appropriate share portfolio or use a computer program (you have to compare; some trackers charge more than others, so you could end up paying different amounts to different managers just to track the same index).

WHEN COSTS ARE CRUCIAL

Costs take on crucial importance when you start to think long-term investment-say in your 30s beginning to build a portfolio for your retirement. Imagine a £50,000 investment which grows at 7% a year over 30 years-now see how returns differ:

LOW-COST TRACKER   £287,000
TYPICAL UK EQUITY TRUST £171,000
FUND OF FUNDS   £121,000

These figures underline how small differences become very big ones when compounded over time. They also show, with share and unit trust yields at the lower end of the 5-10% range, just how much costs matter.

TRACKERS BEAT MANAGERS

If you buy a low-cost tracker, will you lose out on performance? The evidence shows the opposite-because fund managers, taken together, find it difficult to beat the index. There are outstanding fund managers and successful banks (not always the same ones) but the average picture over 20 years tells the story:

44 out of 55 UK managed funds failed to beat the London all-share index. While the all-share index grew at an annual 8.39% the UK equity fund sector grew at only 7.33%. You would have been significantly better off leaving your assets invested in the index.

NOW LOW-COST MANAGEMENT

One reason for this difference lies in the unit trusts' own costs-which is probably why banks such as Schroders and JP Morgan have introduced low-cost managed funds. Dealing costs in London are high, including stamp duty, while more elaborate official rules mean more expensive compliance. And as mathematics demonstrates, it is possible for everyone to beat the average.

Some people still prefer active fund management to the trackers' passive style-when a company joins the index, the tracker has to buy the shares whatever the manager may think about the company's prospects. Large-scale investors will index the core of their portfolio and then feel able to follow some riskier, but potentially more rewarding, ideas.

For the average personal, or retail, investor the tracker trust has to be a leading choice.

****

12

PAY TAX? JUST FLIP IT

Thinking that you may have to sell the holiday flat? Worried about the bill you will get for capital gains tax? Just flip it- one busy flipper in recent years was the then Chancellor of the Exchequer, Alistair Darling. What was good for him, and for many other MPs in the last Parliament, is definitely good enough for you.

You are liable to pay capital gains tax (CGT) whenever you sell something for more than you paid for it-or when you give it away ('disposal' in the taxman's jargon). Every year, there is a tax-free allowance, fixed at £10,600 for 2012-13. If your gains come below this figure, you pay no tax.

18/28% TO PAY

If your gains amount to more than that, you pay a basic 18% tax, which rises to 28% if your gains take you into higher-rate tax. Your gain is added to your income; if all that totals up to £42,475 or more this year (£41,450 next year) you pay the higher rate. This means that any sizeable gain is liable to hit you with tax at 28%.

Most gains and gifts are caught by CGT-but not your house ('main residence') or your car (nor your boat or caravan). If you are married or in a civil partnership, you are allowed to have only one main residence between the two of you (a couple living together, who have no connection in the eyes of HMRC, can have one each). Your holiday flat is liable to tax, but this is where flipping comes in.

Remember, if you have to pay CGT, you can offset the costs of maintenance and the costs of selling-advertising, fees to estate agents, etc. When you sell your main home, you pay no CGT-your main home is where you live

THREE YEARS SAVED

If you live in your holiday flat or second home at any stage, even only for a matter of weeks, it then becomes your main residence and you can write off the last three years' capital gains when you come to sell (the original idea was to help people who had to move house for their job). You have to decide which will be your main home within two years of buying one of your two properties. Once you have made your choice, you can change it- even several times, like the clever Mr Darling. That is flipping- a perfectly legal way to pay less CGT.

GIFTS COUNT, TOO

Most people run into bills for CGT because they make profits by selling shares and unit trusts. Remember that gifts also count-to the taxman, they are sales made at the current market value. So when you decide give your young nephew a parcel of unit trusts when he goes to university (from age 18 he has his own tax allowances) you need first to work out your tax bill.

You will pay tax on the difference between today's value and the original cost- the longer you have held the units, the more you are likely to pay. This amounts to paying tax on price inflation over the years.

If you make a loss when you sell, you can offset this against gains which you have made. Alternatively, you can carry the loss forward to future years. But remember that you will not be allowed to use losses where the gains do not count for CGT. If you lose money selling your boat, you will get no help from the taxman.

GO JOINT?

You need to think about the ownership of any asset where the sale could be hit by CGT. You and your partner each have the £10,600 allowance, so joint ownership of a holiday flat, shares or unit trusts raises the tax- free level to £21, 200.

Children have their own allowances, so each child adds a further £10,600 free from CGT.

You may decide, when you think of selling your unit trusts, that the best idea is to gift half to your partner. You gain the benefit of a doubled tax-free allowance, but you need to do a sum on the amount of tax. In a marriage or civil partnership, a gift ranks as a 'spousal gift' and your partner takes over the original cost which you paid.

A gift made between formally unconnected partners is treated differently. In that case the cost is reckoned as the market value at the time the gift was made. With a shorter time-frame, this is likely to produce a smaller CGT bill than a gift made between spouses or civil partners.

PUT IT TO WORK

The CGT-free allowance is good each year, but you need to put it to work. Suppose that, some years ago, you inherited shares from your father, which are now showing a large gain. You could sell some shares each year, keeping the gains just below the tax-free level. In this way, you would raise the base cost of the shares each year-so reducing your CGT bill when you decide to sell them all.

Once you have sold the shares, you could just buy them back. The shares would still be the same, but would have a higher base cost (this used to be called 'bed and breakfast'). Alternatively, if the shares have fallen, you would have established a loss for CGT. This could be useful one day.

30 DAYS TO WAIT

The snag is that you now have to wait 30 days between selling and buying back-and a lot can happen in the stock market during that time. There are several ways round this; your spouse or civil partner could buy the shares which you sold ('bed and spouse').

You could put your shares into an ISA ('bed and ISA'). You could put the shares into your pension plan ('bed and SIPP').

Or you could simply buy another similar investment. If you were selling an index tracker unit trust, buy one from another management group.

WHEN A BID COMES

One of the reasons people pay CGT is that they cannot help it. What happens is that their shares or unit trusts are bought out. Even if they did not wait to sell, this ranks as a disposal in the eyes of the taxman, so he may want some CGT.

When you hold shares, some other business may launch a cash take-over bid for the company (think Kraft bidding for Cadbury). You may have only a couple of months in which to decide- it generally makes sense to take the money and pay the CGT rather than stay as a small minority shareholder with limited ability to sell. You may be offered the choice of shares or cash, for you to mix and match (especially if the bidder comes from the UK). In that case, you have to do a sum. You should choose just enough cash to stay below the tax-free limit (21,200 this year if the shares are owned jointly with your partner) and take the rest in shares (the deals are often structured for the big investors, such as pension funds which do not pay any CGT).

OR A FUND WINDS UP

When you hold unit trusts, you can be bought out if the management company decides to close them down. Some of the major banks have closing specialist funds which they found had become too small to be economic.

You may be offered a share-for-share swap into another fund. In that case, you will avoid CGT and simply transfer the cost data over to your new investment. Generally, the fund is just wound up, so you get cash and maybe a bill for CGT.

HOW TO DEFER

If you are facing a large bill for CGT, there are ways to defer payment by using the Enterprise Investment Scheme and Seed Enterprise Investment Scheme. (these are both covered in the chapter on tax-efficient investment).

Investing in EIS or SEIS means that you can defer a CGT liability on any asset- and you can go on deferring if you make further EIS or SEIS investments. We all know that a debt deferred is a debt reduced-so long as you do not let tax deferral or tax reduction become the driver of your investment planning.

ESCAPE CGT

Your main home, your car and boat or caravan all escape CGT- and there are other exemptions which could come in useful:

- Personal belongings, 'chattels', sold for less than £6,000 (take care-is that antique chair part of a valuable set?)
- Assets with a useful life of under 50 years-so boats and caravans are exempt.
- Gambling wins, including the pools and lotteries.
- ISAs- so long as you have stayed within the rules.

- UK government stock-known as gilt-edge.
- Shares in Enterprise Investment Scheme, Seed Enterprise Investment Scheme and Venture Capital Trusts.
- Gifts to charity-so if you are planning to make a gift, donate a share which carries a heavy CGT liability.

There is a special Entrepreneur's Relief which limits CGT to 10% on up to £10 million made on disposals of business assets (the top amount was doubled last April). This is a lifetime limit-if you think you might qualify, you will need professional advice.

Finally, there is no CGT on death. If you inherit shares from your spouse which carried a heavy CGT liability, you simply inherit them at their market value, so wiping out the previous gains.

****

13

YOU WILL NEED A PENSION

Planning to retire soon-maybe buy an annuity? Stop!

If you are a man reading this, you may need to move fast. If you are a woman, it may be best to decide to do nothing.

Men's annuity rates are about to drop, while women's rates are expected to improve.

The European Union is shaking up the world of annuities. From 21 December 2012 EU rules lay down that men and women must be offered the same annuity rate. This is their new 'unisex' law.

13% DROP

At present, men's pension incomes are higher than women's because men do not live as long- this is true throughout the world, not just the UK and Europe. Quoting one annuity rate for men and women means that men's rates will fall. The Treasury estimates that male annuity rates could drop by as much as 13%. So any man thinking of buying an annuity in the near future needs to think fast and maybe act sooner rather than later.

Women need to think exact opposite. As their annuity rates are expected to improve, any woman who is working and wondering whether to buy an annuity could be well advised to wait until 2013. By then, thanks to the EU, women will no longer receive smaller annuities than men just because they typically (in the UK) live five years longer.

GILT QUESTION

All this assumes that no other factors will affect annuities over the next few months. The UK's own official rules might alter, but one question mark has to be over the longer-dated, i.e. 15 year, gilt-edged market. Annuity rates are based on long-term gilt-edged yields-it is the drastic fall in these yields over the last five years which has done so much damage to annuities. A rate change, rather up or down, over the next few months would add another significant factor into this equation.

STAKEHOLDER FOR ALL

When you start to plan your pension, many people will tell you that you need to receive an income to see any cash benefit. Not so! Anyone with any size of income, or even no income at all, can set up a pension for themselves or for anybody else-and still get a present of £60 a month from the taxman.

TAXMAN SENDS £720

You are looking at the stakeholder pension. Even if the person who benefits has no income-.your partner at home looking after young kids-you can set up a pension costing £3,600 a year. You will pay £2,880 and taxman sends the other £720 to the insurance company.

This is the only time you can get a tax benefit from a pension contribution without paying any tax and without having any income. Even better, you can set up pensions for your partner, your children, your invalid mother, and every £100 of pension assets will cost just £80. Most people in the UK are eligible for a stakeholder.

WAIT FOR 55

This is how you can make money out of the tax and pension set-up. It is all made easier because there are official limits to the charges, it is easy to move the pension and you are also free to stop and start as you choose. A stakeholder behaves just like any other pension, so you can take 25% tax-free cash when you start to draw down at age 55 or above. You can link pensions with IHT savings, when grandparents set up pension for their grandchildren. This is what you get:

- Each policy brings in the £720 official subsidy;
- The £2,880 a year saves IHT as it is a regular payment which does not affect living standards;
- The grandchildren get a good start to building their own pensions-though, like everyone else, they can only draw their pension from age 55.

Taking out a stakeholder pension has to be a good move- there are not many ways to get £720 a year out of HM Government. But it is clear that a stakeholder is going to meet only a small part of your pension needs when you come to retire.

£50,000 THE MAX

You can invest up to £50,000 a year into a pension and get tax relief, and most people contribute between 10% and 20% of their salary. The key question for so many of us- how to turn these contributions into a decent pension when we retire?

First decision; what do you regard as a decent pension? The conventional answer is that you will need between half and two-thirds of your pre-retirement income -50% probably the minimum while 67% should on average meet most of your needs. Your second decision has to be – how do you get there?

At this point, you have to face the massive change which has complicated pensions over recent years- the virtual end of final salary (defined benefit) pension schemes for new entrants and their replacement by money purchase (defined contribution) plans. This change has shifted the risk in pensions from the employer onto you.

In many cases, employers also trimmed the amount of their contributions when they made the change- which was initially driven by falling annuity rates and the impact on pension plans of people living longer.

NO CERTAINTY

Under the old final salary, you would be paid a proportion of your salary depending how long you had worked for the company. Under defined contribution, you pension will depend on how much went into the pot, how the assets performed and where annuity rates stand when you draw your pension. You have no certainty- you are to a significant degree at the mercy of financial markets when you come to retire.

This loss of certainty worries people, and you will probably be contacted over the next few months over various government ideas to build some guarantee into defined contribution schemes- the new 'defined ambition' pensions. The plan is for the government to give employers a tax incentive if they offer certainty in the form of a minimum pension or a basic cash amount when you retire- some companies already offer a guaranteed income from a defined contribution pension but only if you agree to work until age 70 or 75.

10% AVERAGE

The first clue to what you get out of your pension pot when you retire will be how much you put in. Today, experts reckon that employers put in an average 6% while employees add an average 4%- making total contributions 10%.

This is rather better than the auto-enrolment scheme NEST (National Employment Savings Trust) which is just starting- there the numbers are 4% and 3% plus 1% from the government through tax relief, making a total 8%. (none of this applies to a fifth of the workforce who are civil servants- their index- linked pensions come from the tax payer)

BUT IS 10% ENOUGH?

But will this be enough? Suppose someone starts a job at the UK average salary, doubles it over his working life- and over 40 years he and his employer together put in 10% yearly contributions.

The experts calculate that when he retires, including the state pension, he will get only about one- third of his pre-retirement income. Unless he has other assets, he is facing pensioner poverty.

To get a decent pension when you retire (between a half and two-thirds of what you used to earn) you need to raise this 10% to between 15% and 20%. That is the UK's (and other countries) pension problem; an average pay-in of 10% over someone's working life will not provide sufficient income in retirement- and many people will find that out only when it is too late.

GET A THREE-FIFTHS PENSION

Raising the annual pension contribution from 10% to 15% over 40 years would give a pension almost exactly equal to half of earnings. Pushing the contribution rate up to 20% would give a three-fifths pension when you retire, which would be satisfactory for most of us- many people will be getting less.

Now you can understand why the pension professionals come across as pessimistic. What can you, as a potential pensioner, do about it? You cannot do anything about future annuity rates. You probably have to face an unchanged pension contribution from your employer while you would find it hard to save much more. But there is a way forward- how you handle your pension pot while you are still employed, and the choices you make when you come to retire.

SET UP A SIPP?

For many people, the way to handle your pension pot while you are working is to set up a SIPP –a self- invested personal pension.

The traditional way to build up a pension was to pay an insurance company, or your own employer might be prepared to manage your money in the company pension fund along with everybody else's. The great advantage of a SIPP is that you are in control, you decide which assets are bought and sold and when. (You could even set up a SIPP for your stakeholder plan)

The SIPP is treated just like any other pension fund, and your SIPP supplier will act as joint trustee. His job will be to make sure that your investment policy stays within the rules, but the scope for investment is wide enough for most people- any share list on a recognised exchange, authorised unit trust and most unauthorised trusts, even gold bullion. The main exclusions are residential property and more exotic investments such as stamps and fine wine.

KEEP COSTS DOWN

Because you are in control of the SIPP, you can arrange to keep the costs down. This means doing some homework before you choose the SIPP supplier, but you should not face any costs over setting up the SIPP or when you make contributions. Costs will arise when you buy shares or unit trusts, so you could look at a SIPP operated by one of the discount brokers. If you want advice, as opposed to execution-only, expect to pay.

As you build your pension through a SIPP, or one of the alternative routes, you will see the vital importance of tax-deductibility. All your contributions up to £50,000 a year can be set against tax (assuming your income is at least as large) which is why a SIPP will outperform a similar tax-free ISA for anyone paying tax at 40% or more. People buy ISAs because you can access your money: you cannot get at your pension until age 55.

Tax-deductibility, combined with the ability to cash in 25% of your pension pot, can give you impressive benefits:

- A 40% taxpayer, who is age 60 and about to retire, puts £10,000 into a pension policy;
- He gets £4,000 tax relief;
- He cashes in 25% of his policy, or £2,500;
- He now has a policy for £7,500 which has cost him a net £3,500;
- An insurance company offers him an annuity of £435. (this is before the EU's unisex rules!)

A return of £435 on a spend of £3,500 represents a yield of just under 12.5%. In today's financial climate, this is a truly amazing (and safe) return- mainly because pension contributions are tax-deductible.

YOUR FINAL CHOICE

So you come up to retirement. You have a satisfactory pension pot, thanks to a low-cost and successful SIPP, and you have set up stakeholder plans for your relatives. All looks good-you have one final important decision to make. Do you buy an annuity or do you choose the alternative, known as income drawdown?

One choice you no longer have to make is to decide by age 75- nowadays you can leave your pension fund untouched as long as you like.

When you decide to retire at age 55 or later, you will probably take 25% as tax-free cash. You cannot get your hands on the cash unless you buy an annuity or start income drawdown- if you decide not to take cash you are not allowed to change your mind later on. And you cannot reinvest the cash back into your pension fund.

A SIMPLE ANNUITY?

What do you choose? An annuity is essentially simple- you specify whether you want a level income, or build-in increases and whether you want to leave a part-annuity to your partner. You also need to think about impaired annuities.

People who smoke, have health problems or demanding jobs can get better annuity rates.

Annuity income is secure: whatever happens in the financial world-once you have set up an annuity it cannot be altered. Unless you buy a guarantee, your annuity will die with you.

Income drawdown is fundamentally different. You take your 25% cash, and draw your income direct from your pension fund. The fund stays invested, and you remain in control and you make all the investment decisions. The government lays down the maximum income you can take, but there is no minimum- just zero.

OR A TYPE OF DRAWDOWN?

There are two types of drawdown, depending on your financial situation. In income, or capped, drawdown the maximum income you can take is roughly equal to an annuity. As long as you stay within the maximum, you can take what amount you like when you like.

Flexible drawdown, the second type, is available to people who have a secure pension income of at least £20,000 a year. Investment income or income from property does not count. Under the flexible drawdown, there are no income limits. You are free to draw as much income as you want, when you want it (the government reckons that, even if your flexible drawdown turns into a disaster, the secure £20,000 a year means that you will not become a burden on the social services).

FREEDOM AT A PRICE

You get freedom with both types of drawdown, but you need to appreciate that this comes at a price. Once you take an annuity, there is nothing further to pay. Under both types of drawdown, you will pay administration plus investment management costs-higher on the more complex flexible drawdown- and financial advice will cost if you need it. On the plus side, you can pass any remaining pension to your beneficiaries, though there will be 55% tax to pay. The appeal of drawdown is that it puts you in the driving seat- which also represents the big risk, especially in income drawdown. If you make bad investment decisions, your capital and your retirement pension will suffer, especially if you draw the maximum income from the drawdown fund. You are free anytime to switch your drawdown to an annuity.

MINIMUM MAKES SENSE
The combination of running costs and risk means that a pension fund should probably reach a minimum size before you consider

drawdown- maybe £250,000 depending on your other assets and income. Flexible drawdown will appeal to the better off, where their basic living costs are covered and they can use part of their pension to buy the secure £20,000 income which is required.

For many people attracted by drawdown, the answer for their retirement will be a compromise-a 50-50 split between drawdown and a traditional annuity. Take the case of someone who chose drawdown in 2000. They would have had a torrid twelve years since then, losing a large slice of the original capital and seeing their maximum income drop by around 50%. The man who took out an annuity would have received a trouble-free pension about twice as large.

One scenario has to be; cover your living costs through an annuity and invest the rest of your pension pot in a more flexible drawdown- being all the time aware that you could lose part, in theory all, of your drawdown capital.

****

14

TAXING YOU LATER..........

You will get no benefit at all when you plan to reduce Inheritance Tax (IHT) Saving IHT will help your surviving partner, your children and dependants.

IHT is charged on what you leave as your estate. The taxman pulls all the assets together and then deducts the debts such as a mortgage or a charge for equity release. Be aware that all assets mean everything you own anywhere in the world- including that time-share in the Canaries- and holdings such as ISAs which were previously tax-free. Your own home represents the largest item in most people's estate.

40% ABOVE THE BAND

The taxman then does a simple sum. If your estate totals less than £325,000, which marks the nil rate band, there is no IHT to pay. Everything above that figure is taxed at 40%, the same as higher rate income tax. The theory is simple; if your estate comes out at £375,000, the excess over the nil rate band is £50,000 on which

40% tax will amount to £20,000. The tax will have to be paid upfront before anyone can access what you left.

Leaving money to your spouse or civil partner represents the biggest break in IHT. (Couples who live together have no such benefit) Suppose you leave £325,000, i.e. the nil rate band, to your children and everything else to your spouse. In that case, no IHT would have to be paid-though the spouse who survived might later have to pay more IHT as their estate has been increased.

This is where you need to do some sums before you decide. (Transfers free from IHT work even if the spouses are separated- but stops working when they divorce)

SHARE THE REST

Many people just leave everything to their spouse- there may not be any close dependants, or the surviving spouse may be the one who needs the money. To the extent the nil rate band is not used, it can pass to the one who is left. So if everything goes to the spouse, none of the nil rate band will be used, and the survivor will then have a £650,000 nil rate band to reduce the tax value of their estate. Sharing the nil rate band can be backdated, up to 40 years. If your spouse died say five years ago, and did not claim all of their nil rate band then you can make use of the difference. Just remember that HMRC will want to see all the documentation- death certificate, grant of probate and so on.

MAKE A WILL

How do you reduce the size of your estate, so that your family will have to pay less IHT? The first step is to make a will. It is important that you direct where your assets are distributed- and not just for tax reasons. If you do not make a will, i.e. you die intestate, the rules for intestacy may apply and override what you intended.

The surviving widow or widower may get less and some money may have to go to relatives you would not have included. For partners who are not married nor in a civil partnership, making a will is essential. (Go to a solicitor-your DIY version could be challenged)

SLIDING SCALE

The way most people reduce their estate is by giving things away. When you make a gift, it will escape IHT altogether seven years after it is made. There is some benefit after three years, when a sliding scale operated. The taxman will start by adding all your gifts to the estate, but only 80% after three to four years, 60% for four to five, 40% for five to six, and 20% for six to seven.

When you do make gifts, it is worth considering a life policy. Your aim is to cover the IHT liability which would fall on the person who receives the gift in case you die within seven years. So you would probably go for a reducing term policy. It may be possible to arrange for the estate to pick up the bill for IHT-though this could raise questions of fairness among the people who inherit.

GIVE IT AWAY

Certain types of gifts are built into the system. You can give away £3,000 a year to anyone you choose and carry the allowance over for a further year. Spouses and civil partners each have the allowance, so between the two they could give away £12,000 if neither has used the allowance from the previous tax year. You can also give up to £250 in each tax year to any number of different people so long as they have not received any other gift from you.

Gift to charity are also exempt from IHT, as is money which is spent on your child's education or to look after a dependent relative. There is a special range of wedding gifts, from £1,000 by anyone up to £5,000 given by each partner.

FROM YOUR NORMAL SPEND

You are allowed to make any number of gifts out of your normal expenditure. These are gifts made out of your after-tax income which do not affect your standard of living-so you do not have to draw on capital to make these gifts.

Investors are also given some exemptions from IHT, notably shares listed on the Alternative Investment Market (AIM) once these have been held for two years. AIM has grown into a major market, with more than 3,000 companies-the scope is wide, and IHT exemption represents a useful plus. Investments you make in Enterprise and Seed Enterprise Investment Schemes also come free of IHT after two years (see the previous chapter).

This year, there is a new tax break for people who leave part of their estate to charity. If you give away at least 10% to charity, your heirs get a 10% reduction in the IHT rate. This means that the estate above £325,000 will be taxed at 36% rather than the standard 40%

GIFTS MUST BE REAL

Many gifts, particularly in the family, come as objects rather than money- paintings or maybe even a holiday flat or second home. This is an area containing some nasty trip-wires.

The first essential is that your gift must be 100% genuine- what the lawyers call an absolute gift, irrevocable, free and unencumbered. Otherwise, you may be said to have made a gift 'with reservation' which to HMRC does not count as a gift at all. If I give my daughter a Spanish holiday flat, I have to pay her a market rental if I go to stay. The taxman will pounce even if there is just an understanding and no formal agreement-say if you give the house to your son but you continue to live there.

Even if your gift is genuine, another trip-wire sits in wait- POAT, or the Pre Owned Assets Test. If you think you might have a POAT problem, you will need professional advice. The theory is that you have to pay tax if you benefit from an asset which you previously owned back to 1986!

The classic example: in that year you gave your son a parcel of shares in Apple, which made him a lot of money. As a thank-you, he puts down the deposit on your new flat. You are caught for POAT!

THREE AREAS FOR HELP

More people are now looking at substantial bills for IHT, partly because of rising house prices in London and the south-east. If you reckon that the family could face an IHT liability running into six figures, it is time to think about some special measures. There are three principal areas which could help.

Trusts are the traditional answer- they have been used for hundreds of years to protect family wealth. Successive governments have tightened the rules, so that now you will be hit by a 20% tax charge for any gifts made into trust which go over the £325,000 nil rate band.

USE THE RULES

You have to survive for another seven years or a further 20% will fall due. This should provide some help, and there are ways to cope with this problem by using the IHT rules. You could make regular gifts out of income, pay these into the trust and avoid the immediate charge for IHT. Every seven years, you can make tax-free gifts to the trust up to the value of the nil rate band.

If you decide to use trusts, you will definitely need professional help- not just to follow the complex rules but to decide which sort of trust will deliver what you looking for. If you want to keep access to your capital, but are prepared to give away the future growth, you should probably think of a loan trust. If you are prepared to lose access to your capital, but still need the income, then consider a discounted gift trust.

FAMILY PARTNERSHIP

Trusts have other advantages- they make it easier to handle someone's estate- but the tougher official rules have led people to look elsewhere. One alternative is the family limited partnership (FLP). This set- up avoids the 20% IHT tax in a trust when you

126

transfer more than the nil rate band. The FLP, which will probably be owned by trust, operates as a business and has no fixed life.

A transfer into a FLP counts as a 'potentially exempt transfer' which means that you have to survive for seven years to escape any IHT. If you go down this route it may be sensible to think about term life assurance.

BUSINESS RELIEF

Another centuries–old way of avoiding IHT has been to invest in agricultural property-more recently in business property, where reliefs mean that no IHT will be due on land and buildings, plant, stock and so on. The next step was for professionals to set up business property funds which would deliver 100% relief from IHT once you have owned the investment for two years (and it forms part of the estate).

It has even proved possible for these funds to generate some income. Your assets could be unquoted shares.

CONTROL ISSUE

An IHT fund along these lines offer major advantages over the traditional type of trust. You have to make gifts into a trust, and so lose immediate control of your assets. In the business property fund you stay in control and may be able to make withdrawals.

A conventional trust can take up to seven years to become fully effective, while the business property fund becomes operational five years quicker. One issue in a business property fund is likely to be the size of the investment- you may be looking at a minimum subscription of around £50,000. You also have to recognise, in the current climate, that schemes of this kind may be singled out for attack by HMRC.

YOU NEED PLAN B

You plan to deal with the IHT when the head of the family dies, but perhaps it all misfires. Maybe the savings route had to be changed, maybe the papers were not signed in time. You find yourself back to square one; what is Plan B? The short answer is a deed of variation- you will need a solicitor to draw up the deed. Within two years of someone's death, you can rewrite their will so long as all the beneficiaries agree- though you are not allowed to compensate someone who gives up a benefit. When you rewrite, you could save IHT by giving a bigger legacy to the surviving widow/widower or by donating money to his favourite charity, or you could set up a trust.

In this situation, people arrange to skip a generation by giving the money to the patriarch's grandchildren rather than his grown-up sons and daughters (if children under age 18 are involved, you may need approval from the court). You can even arrange a deed of variation if he did not leave a will. A deed of variation is an effective Plan B, but many people prefer prevention to cure.

GLOSSARY- WHAT FINANCIAL TERMS MEAN

Absolute Return Fund: a fund which aims to make a positive return whether the stock market rises or falls. Some funds charge a performance fee.

Basis Points: how the markets describe interest rates, where 100 basis points equal 1%

BRIC: term coined to refer to the four major emerging-market economies- Brazil, Russia, India, China.

CPI: consumer prices index, now used by the government rather than RPI, the retail prices index. CPI excludes housing costs.

Carry Trade: borrow in a currency where interest rates are low (often Japan) to lend in a currency where rates are high (typically Europe) Currency fluctuations can make this risky.

Chapter 11: Bankruptcy protection in the US. A company's obligations to its creditors are postponed, giving it time to reorganise.

Collateratalised Debt Obligation (CDO): a financial structure which groups bonds and other debts into a portfolio which can then be traded. In theory, the spread of risk should improve the credit rating.

Credit Default Swap: a type of financial insurance. The buyer of the swap pays the seller in return for protection if a loan defaults.

Credit Rating Agency: companies such as Standard & Poor, Moody's, Fitch, which publish ratings on debt issued by companies and countries. Changes in the ratings of countries' loans featured in the Eurozone debt crisis.

Current/Running Yield: the current level of income expressed as a percentage of the bond or share price.

Default: when a company, or a country, fails to meet the interest or re-payment obligations which are due on its debt. Default may have to be decided by court or a tribunal-as happened to Greece.

Deleveraging: reducing the amount of borrowings- as government and individuals have been doing in the UK.

Derivatives: assets whose value is fixed by reference to (so derived from) other assets. Options to buy shares represent a basic derivative.

Double Dip: when an economy, which had been in recession, recovers but then slips back (as it would appear when drawn on a chart).

Equity Release: a way to realise the value of your house (net of debt)-often by a lifetime mortgage, where the interest is rolled up.

Futures: a futures contract is an agreement to buy or sell currency or a commodity at a pre-arranged date and price. Can be used to hedge or speculate.

GDP: gross domestic product. Measures the economic activity in a country.

Gross Redemption Yield: the yield, generally on a bond, which takes into account the gain or loss over the buying price if the bond is held to maturity.

Hedge Funds: these aim to make money whatever the stock market conditions, e.g. by investing in commodities as well as shares and by using financial assets such as derivatives.

Identity Theft: when a criminal finds out your personal details and uses these to buy goods and get credit cards and a passport.

Impaired Life Annuities: annuities offering a better rate than average to people who smoke, work in strenuous occupations or have a history of illness.

Junk Bond: a bond which carries a high rate of interest to compensate the buyer for a higher risk of default. Junk is the lowest credit rating, currently applied to Greece.

LIBOR: London Inter Bank Offered Rate: The rate at which banks lend money to one another.

Lifestyle Option: when an insurance company or an adviser moves investments from shares into cash and bonds as the beneficiary approaches retirement.

Monetary Policy Committee: the Bank of England group which meets to fix the level of Bank Rate.

Money Laundering: moving money made from crime into the mainstream financial system.

Option: an agreement which gives the right, but not the obligation, to buy or sell an asset at a pre-agreed price at a pre-agreed time. You can walk away from an option, simply letting it lapse.

PIGS: countries in the Eurozone with debt problems- Portugal, Ireland, Greece, Spain. Question now whether Italy should be included.

Ponzi scheme: a fraud where dividends paid not out of profits but from the capital invested by new shareholders. Bernie Madoff ran the biggest-ever Ponzi scheme. (Charles Ponzi was a US operator in the 1920s)

Quantitative Easing (QE): when the Bank of England puts credit into the banking system by buying assets such as government bonds. Major risk is that QE will push up inflation.

Recession: when income or output declines for two successive quarters.

Retail Price Index (RPI); the traditional measure of price inflation for consumers (see CPI)

Securitisation: when a variety of debts (mortgages, credit card debit, student loans) are packaged together in a company whose shares can be traded.

Short selling: when an investor borrows shares to sell, aiming to buy them back more cheaply when they fall- and so make his profit.

Stagflation: the difficult combination of low growth and price inflation- as in the UK during 2011-12.

Sub Prime: housing loans made to borrowers with a poor financial history (the borrowers are called ninjas-no income, no job, no assets).

Tier 1 Capital: test of a bank's strength, through the amount of its shares, disclosed reserved and retained profits.

Toxic Debt: loans made by banks which are unlikely to be repaid in full- or maybe not repaid at all. Toxic debts can be hived off into 'bad banks' (in the US, toxic debt is sometimes called 'legacy assets')

Warrant: a document giving the right to buy a share at a stated price at a stated time- like an option, but warrants are often listed separately on the stock market.

Write- Down: reducing the balance sheet value of an asset to bring it into line with the market or to reflect a changed situation.

Yield Gap: the difference in yield between shares and bonds- regarded as a guide to stock market prospects.

.

Useful Addresses

Association of Investment Trust Companies (AITC)
Durrant House
8-13 Chiswell Street
London EC1Y 4YY
Hotline: 020 7282 5555
www.aitc.co.uk

Debt Management Office
Eastcheap Court
11 Philpot Lane
London EC3M 8UD
Tel: 0845 357 6500
www.dmo.gov.uk

Department for Work and Pensions (DWP)
If you ring The Pension Service on 0845 606 0265,
You will be connected to the pension centre covering you area,
Or you can look on the website (www.
thepensionservice.gov.uk/contact)

You can obtain DWP leaflets from Pension Service and
Jobcentre Plus office and some post offices, CABs or
Libraries.

You can write to:

Pension Guides
Freepost
Bristol BS38 7WA
Tel: 08457 31 32 33

If you have access to the Internet, you can download the leaflets (and claim forms for many of the benefits) from www.dwp.gov. uk or www.thepensionservice.gov.uk

Financial Ombudsman
Service (FOS)
South Quay Plaza
183 Marsh Wall
London E14 9SR
Consumer helpline: 0845 080 1800
www.financialombudsman.org.uk

Financial Services Authority (FSA)
25 The North Colonnade
Canary Wharf
London E14 5HS
Consumer helpline: 0845 606 1234
www.fsa.gov.uk/consummer

HM Revenue & Customs (HMRC)
The government department that deals
With al;most all the taxes due in the UK.
Most HMRC leaflets can be obtained
From local tax offices or Tax Enquiry Centres
(look for in the phone book under `Revenue'
or `Government Department') or Jobcentre Plus offices.
Almost all are also available on the website at:
www.hmrc.gov.uk or you can ring them the Orderline:
Tel: 0845 900 0404

HM Revenue & Customs National Insurance
Contributions Office (NICO)
Benton Park View

Newcastle upon Tyne NE98 1ZZ
Enquiry Line: 0845 302 1479

International Pension Centre
The Pension Service
Tyneview Park
Newcastle upon Tyne NE98 1BA
Tel: 01912 187777
(8.00am-8.00pm,weekdays)

Investment Management Association
65 Kingsway
London WC2B 6TD
Tel: 020 7831 0898
020 7269 4667
www.investmentfunds.org.uk
(OEIC.S).

MoneyFACTS
MoneyFacts House
66-70 Thorpe Road
Norwich NR1 1BJ
Tel: 01603 476 178
www.moneyfactsgroup.co.uk

The Pension Service
State Pension Forecasting Team
Future Pension Centre
Tyneview Park
Whitley Road Newcastle upon Tyne NE98 1BA
Tel: 0845 3000 168
www.thepensionservice.gove.uk

Pension Tracing Service

Tel: 0845 600 2537

www.thepensionservice.gov.uk

Pension Advisory Service

(TPAS)
11 Belgrave Road
London SW1V 1RB
Helpline: 0845 601 2923
www.pensionsadvisoryservice.org.uk

Specialist Magazines

Moneyfacts

Moneyfacts House
6-70 Thorpe Road
Norwich NR1 1BJ
0845 1689 600

www.moneyfacts.co.uk
This magazine publishes a monthly round up of all savings account rates. For more up-to-date listings see the web site.

Trade Bodies

The Association of Investment Trust Companies
9th Floor
24 Chiswell Street
London EC1Y 4YY
0207 282 5555
www.itsonline.co.uk www.aitc.co.uk
Provides information on aspects of investing in investment trust companies.

The Investment Management Association
65 Kingsway
London WC2B 6TD
020 7269 4639

www.investmentuk.org
Provides information on investing in unit trusts and Oeics

Proshare
4th Floor Bankside House
107 Leadenhall Street
London EC3A 4AF
0906 802 2222
www.proshare.org.uk

Advises on setting up investment clubs and runs education
programmes for schools on share ownership

The Association of British Insurers
61 Gresham Street
London EC2V 7HQ
020 7600 333
www.abi.org.uk
Publishes information sheets on all aspects of insurance.

The British Insurance Brokers Association
14 Bevis Marks
London EC3A 7NT
0901 814 0015
www.biba.org.uk
www.bsa.org.uk

The Council of Mortgage Lenders
Bush House
North West Wing
Aldwych
London
WC2B 4PJ

0845 373 6771
www.cml.org.uk

Borrowing

The National Debtline
0808 808 4000

The Association of British Credit Unions
Holyoake House
Hanover Street
Manchester M60 OAS
0161 832 8694
www.abcul.org

Credit Information Agencies
Experian
Consumer help services
PO Box 8000
Nottingham NG1 5GX
0870 241 6212
www.experian.com

Equifax Europe (UK)
Credit file advice centre
PO Box 3001

Glasgow G81 0583
0870 010 0583
www.equifax.co.uk

Investment information websites
www.investment-gateway.com
www.new-online-investor.co.uk
www.find.co.uk

Index